ask hayley

REAL ANSWERS FOR TODAY'S TEEN

VOL. 2

Revell
www.revellbooks.com

Hungry Planet
www.hungryplanet.net

contents

on the cover

The planet is hungry. We want to help. Books and resources about your life, for your life.

www.hungryplanet.net

*JIC u cnt rd dis ad: Here at Hungry Planet, it's no big deal. We speak your language. From your boyfriend
to your best friend forever, from school to dating to your parents, relax. We understand you.

Can't live without it? p 36

parents

Embarrassing parents? p 62

boys

god

mean girls

Are you trying to be one? p 30

lifestyle

Want to be the best girlfriend ever? p 32

contents

Guys or gals: who do you hang with? p 102

crisis

friends

extras

What's a shy girl to do? p 70

Say good-bye to the blues! p 132

Hot or not? p 26

Your super hot party dress just totally
got this cute guy's attention.

It got this guy's attention too.
And he has a camera.

You can't control what guys think,
but you can control what you wear.

Are you dressing
too hot?

howhotis2hot.com

Copyright Holder

© 2008 by Hungry Planet

Publisher

Published by Revell
a division of Baker Publishing Group
P.O. Box 6287, Grand Rapids, MI 49516-6287
www.revellbooks.com

Printing

Printed in the United States of America

Cataloging-in-Publication Data

Library of Congress Cataloging-in-Publication Data
DiMarco, Hayley.
    Ask Hayley : real answers for today's teen / Hayley DiMarco.
    p. cm.
    ISBN 978-0-8007-3236-3 (pbk.)
    1. Teenage girls—Conduct of life. 2. Success in adolescence. 3. Teenage
girls—Religious life. I. Title.
BJ1681.D56 2007
646.700835'2—dc22   2007014152

Associations

Published in association with Yates & Yates, LLP, Literary Agents, Orange, California.

Interior Design

Sarah Lowrey Brammeier

Scripture Permissions

Unless otherwise indicated, Scripture is taken from the HOLY BIBLE, NEW INTERNA-
TIONAL VERSION®. NIV®. Copyright © 1973, 1978, 1984 by International Bible
Society. Used by permission of Zondervan. All rights reserved.

Scripture marked NASB is taken from the New American Standard Bible®, Copyright
© 1960, 1962, 1963, 1968, 1971, 1972, 1973, 1975, 1977, 1995 by The Lock-
man Foundation. Used by permission.

Scripture marked GNT is taken from the Good News Translation—Second Edition
Copyright © 1992 by American Bible Society. Used by permission.

Scripture marked NLT is taken from the Holy Bible, New Living Translation, copyright
© 1996. Used by permission of Tyndale House Publishers, Inc., Wheaton, Illinois
60189. All rights reserved.

Portions of this book have been adapted from material in Stupid Parents (Revell, 2006),
The Dirt on Dating (Revell, 2005), Idol Girls (Revell, 2007), Mean Girls (Revell, 2004),
Sexy Girls (Revell, 2006), and Dateable (Revell, 2003).

A Letter from Hayley

Volume Two has arrived! I'm so excited that our chatting just keeps on going. It's great getting to know all of you. Thanks so much for trusting me with such important issues in your life. It sounds like I fried your brain in *Stupid Parents: Why They Just Don't Understand and How You Can Help*. So to clear things up, I've answered several parental questions in this issue. I'm also proud of how much you want to please God even if it seems impossible at times. So I hope you enjoy this issue with its God stuff. And remember as you read it that these other girls are just like you, and that means you are not alone. We are all dealing with some issue or other. None of us is perfect, but we are getting there. So flip around the mag and find the stuff that applies to you. And if one of your very own questions is in here, I hope you enjoy seeing your name in a book. Pretty cool huh? Remember, you can always ask me questions on www.askhayley.com. And who knows, maybe you'll make it into the next issue.

Stay true!

Hayley

it's a date
—what do i do now?

Dear Hayley,

This boy at work who I've liked forever just asked me out. I've always wished he would, but now that he has, I'm scared. I really like this guy and I don't want to mess it up. I've had some miserable dates in the past, and guys don't usually ask me out again. How do I act? What do I say? What do I do? Help me!

Sara

Dear Sara,

Don't panic. Dates are easy, really, if you just remember one thing: he's not a girl! Seems like a no-brainer, but a lot of us forget and treat guys just like our girlfriends. That's when things get messed up. Girls share all their deepest, darkest secrets with one another. We tell our friends *everything*! The good, the bad, and the ugly. And doing that with guys is a disaster. Don't tell him all about everything you are feeling or thinking; it's too much information. That means no complaining, no bragging, no gossiping, no long stories about your childhood. All a guy really wants on a date is a happy, relaxed girl who thinks he's funny and strong and smart. Happy means you like whatever he has planned and don't complain about the little things. Relaxed means you are focusing not on yourself and your fears but on him and his thoughts and feelings. And that means you are listening to him talk, laughing when he jokes, and trusting him to give you a great, fun evening. You do those things and you'll look like a confident and fun girl who he'd love to be with. A first date should be a fun, lighthearted time when all you have to do is enjoy his company, not identify your soul mate!

Hayley

12 Ways To Be tHe BeSt DaTe EveR

Don't offer to meet him somewhere.
Let him come and get you. He loves that part.

Let him plan the date.
Some guys have no idea how to do this, but they should. If he asks, he plans. If he doesn't plan, then you can make a suggestion, but don't take that role away from him if he is man enough to step into it.

Make conversation,
but if he is really nervous and talks about himself the entire time, don't get upset. That's just his way of telling how much of a catch he is and how much he wants to prove to you that he's worthy of you. By the second date he should be more calm and open to hearing from you.

Let him get your chair.
A true gentleman will pull out your chair for you and slowly push it in as you sit down. Smile and say thank you.

If he is talking too much,
don't ask him a lot of questions. He doesn't bond by talking like you do, so if you think that asking him questions makes him like you more, you are wrong. It just makes him like himself more. Let him ask you questions, and if he doesn't then feel free to just interrupt him to make comments on what he is saying. Guys interrupt each other; that's how they talk. They don't ask questions. So feel free to be part of the convo and cut in. Don't change the subject; just join in.

Slow down and let him get doors.
That's him showing you that he is a gentleman, so don't try to steal that job from him. (Note: If it's a revolving door, let him go in first so he can push it.)

At the movies or theater,

once you two pick the best place, go into the row of seats first.

Eat. Order a sensible meal, meaning one you can eat.

And then eat it. Don't order a steak and then not touch it—oooh, he hates that—or a small salad and water. You eat, so don't pretend you don't. Guys love to see a girl with a good appetite. It's one of the things they find attractive in girls.

Let him pay,

and then say, "Thank you for dinner. That was so nice of you. I loved it." This is a big part of letting him lead. It is a symbol of him as provider and protector. (Note: If you go out with this guy a lot, you can start to offer to pay every so often. But not all the time, and definitely not on the first date.)

Talk about good things.

Don't whine about bad stuff.
And laugh at his jokes (or his attempts at jokes).

Don't reach across and unlock his door.

If you were considered important enough to have your door opened, then you shouldn't then have to reach across and unlock his side, especially if you are nicely dressed. Some guys might think that is unkind of you, but deep down when you do reach across they know that their service to you of opening your door isn't as special.

Don't call him the next day

or even the next week. Let him call you. You are the one who is being chased, not the chaser. Call him first and I guarantee you'll drop 5 points on the hotness scale.

Excerpted from *The Dirt on Dating*

Taboo Topics
for a first Date

Don't talk about . . .

- your ex-boyfriend(s)
- your problems at home
- your cat's health problems
- anything negative

- your health problems
- how much you want to get married
- how much you like him
- how great you are

Excerpted from *The Dirt on Dating*

Your days of wishing
for a manual are over.

A Dateable Book

The *Dirt* on
Dating

Hayley DiMarco

The *Dirt* on
Breaking Up

Hayley DiMarco & Justin Lookadoo

The *Dirt* on
Drugs

Justin Lookadoo

The *Dirt* on
Sex

Justin Lookadoo

It's real. It's raw. It's true. It's the Dirt.

forbidden from
the prom
—why can't i go?

Dear Hayley,

Help! My parents won't let me go to my prom. It's the first year I've been asked, and I really want to go. My mom says I'm too young (I'm a sophomore) and she doesn't want me to go. But all my friends are going, so I should be able to go too, shouldn't I? What can I say to her to convince her that it's okay for me to go?

Bethany

Dear Bethany,

I know how much fun proms can be, and I know how hard it must be to think you can't go. But here's the deal: Your parents are responsible for you. They support you. They pay for all your stuff—your house, your food, everything—and according to the law, they are responsible for your life. For whatever reason, they don't think that going to the prom is good for you. Now, they may be wrong or they may be right, but the truth is, that doesn't matter. You've got to do whatever they say unless they want you to break the law! Now, I can help you to potentially help them change their minds, but what I want you to get is that this might just be an opportunity for you to prove your obedience to them and to God. After all, at home is where you learn how to be faithful even when it hurts. Rules are just a chance for you to learn self-discipline and sanctification, both very godly characteristics.

But that doesn't mean you can't help your parents understand the situation a little better. I'm not telling you to argue with them—that never helps—but educate them if you can. Help them to understand what would happen on prom night. Tell them who you would go with, what you would do, and when you would be home. If possible, you might want to ask them to volunteer to be chaperones at the dance. I know that doesn't sound perfect, but maybe if they chaperoned they would let you go. It's worth a try.

I have a youth pastor friend who had a group prom dinner at their house for their daughter, her date, and three other couples (to minimize costs and be safer). Then the group went to the prom and came back to their house for their "after party." That removed the typical parent fears about booze and hotel rooms.

Whatever the outcome when you talk to your parents, I want you to take it like a woman! Don't whine and complain, because then you'll just prove them right—that you aren't old enough for the prom. Just accept what they say, thank them for listening, and tell them you hope they'll see enough maturity in you next spring. That may just show them a side of you they haven't seen yet. Trust takes lots of time to grow. Start now by proving to them that you aren't a baby and can handle adult decisions, and maybe next time they'll be more lenient.

Hayley

"Trust takes lots of time to grow. Start now by proving to them that you aren't a baby and can handle adult decisions."

How

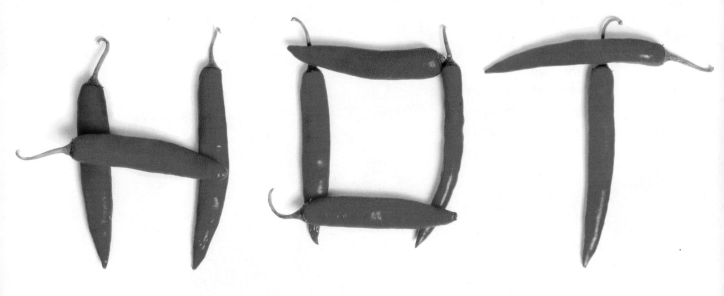

Is **Too Hot?**

When skin is in and it's hard to find anything but skin-tight to wear, how is a girl supposed to know where to draw the line? Find out:

✓ what you are really saying about yourself through your clothes and actions

✓ why little things called hormones affect the way guys look at girls

✓ what words like *modesty* and *purity* really mean

✓ what God thinks about people trying to look and act sexy

Guess what? *Sexy Girls* won the Christian Book Award for best youth book for 2007! So don't let your parents be scared off by the cover—this is good stuff!

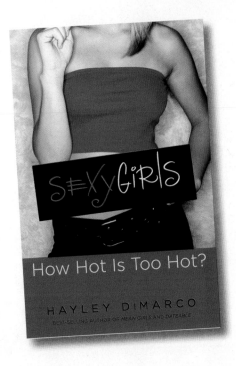

  Available at bookstores everywhere.

www.hungryplanet.net   www.revellbooks.com

i lost my best friend by
**sleeping
with
him**

Dear Hayley,

I have a problem and I don't know who else to talk to about it. Over the summer for some reason I decided that I wasn't good enough to ever be truly loved by anyone, so I looked for love in the wrong places and had sex with one of my friends. It changed me a lot. I lost respect for myself, and even though I knew what I was doing was wrong, I felt like I had to continue doing it. I got scared when my period came late, but he reassured me he wasn't going to leave me. But now he's freaking out and not talking to me.

I don't know what I'm going to do, because I can't tell my parents—they would kill me. Now he says we can't be friends anymore. That scared me more because it seems like whether I'm pregnant or not we won't be friends anymore. How can I get my friend back?

I've prayed about all this and asked for forgiveness but somehow it doesn't feel like anything's changed.

Hailey (with an I)

Dear Hailey,

I'm glad you wrote me. I'm going to do what I can to help you figure this stuff out. First of all, let me explain something about forgiveness. It's easy to be forgiven—all you have to do is confess your sin and accept the forgiveness—but that doesn't mean that you will "feel" any different. What you've been doing is wrong, and when you do wrong stuff, you feel awful. That's normal, and it will pass eventually.

Now we have to deal with the aftermath of your choices. You were old enough to make the decision to have sex, and you are old enough now to deal with the results—potential pregnancy—but it will take a lot of courage. If you are pregnant, then it's no longer all about you but all about the baby growing inside of you. You have to stop thinking about your heartache and pain right now and figure out how to move forward for the baby.

I know it seems like your parents will kill you, but trust me, they won't. Parents don't kill the kids they love, even when they mess up. Now, they will more than likely be disappointed and angry, but they won't physically harm you. The reason you have to tell them is because you can't hide it for long anyway. And you're going to need their help. Being pregnant will be hard, but you can do it. And then you and your parents can decide what to do with the baby. They can either help you raise it or you can make a plan to have the baby adopted by a loving family. But either way, your life is going to change. (And please, no matter what anybody says, don't let them talk you into an abortion. If you think you feel awful right now, imagine how you would feel if you had to live the rest of your life knowing you had killed your baby. It would be unbearable.)

If you don't want to tell your parents until you find out if you're pregnant or not, then I suggest you talk to a youth pastor or counselor at church and see if they can help you get tested. There are crisis pregnancy centers all over the country that will give you a free pregnancy test and help you with talking to your parents. You can get more info at www.pregnancycenters.org.

Now, baby doll, when it comes to the subject of the boy, he's right. You can no longer be friends. You've crossed a line that can't be erased. Each time you are together, you run the risk of doing it again. And you can't risk that. Being friends after having a sexual relationship is really hard, if not impossible. One of the two people will always be hurt when the other finds a mate. It's tragic, but sex ruins a friendship. It sounds like he's not going to marry you to help you raise the baby, and if that's the case, then you've got to move forward with taking care of this on your own. It's awful, and boys shouldn't be so stupid, but they are.

I know what it's like to give up on God and just want to go have fun. I did the very same thing. But when I finally turned around and realized how badly I needed him and how much he loved me, I gave up all that stupid stuff. And life got tons better. It sounds like you know all this stuff and at some point believed it. You just got off track. You started looking inward instead of upward. And that's normal but painful. Looking for fulfillment and love in sex is, as you now know, useless and dangerous. You may or may not be pregnant, but either way, the sex stuff has to stop. And your friend is right: you can't be friends anymore.

So go with a parent or someone from your church to get tested for free right away so you can figure out what the next step really is. You'll at least get a measure of peace knowing one way or the other. Then surround yourself with godly people who will counsel you on becoming the woman God wants you to be, whether with or without a baby.

Hayley

"I know it seems like your parents will kill you, but trust me, they won't."

CAUTION

HOW FAR IS TOO FAR?

In a culture where hookups and friends-with-benefits are commonplace, it can be hard to know what to do about guys, love, romance, and sex. Find out:

- How far is too far
- How to seek God's forgiveness
- How to get back on track

i'm sick of being
called a tease

Dear Hayley,
I'm sick of being called a tease. The boys at school always say that, and I don't get it. I'm not easy, I don't sleep around, in fact, I've never even had a boyfriend. Why are they so mean? I just want to be good and not mess up sexually, so why do they treat me like I'm a tease? That's something sexual, right?

Shelley

Dear Shelley,

I'm so proud of you for wanting to be pure and not mess up sexually, but it sounds like you might be missing the mark when it comes to your sexuality. See, staying pure is more than just not having sex. It's also watching what you do to the thought life of the guys around you. If they are calling you a tease, that means that in some way or another, you are teasing them—taunting them into thinking they can get you sexually—but then you reject them. And that's not purity.

There are two ways that you could be teasing boys. One is by flirting with them so much that it leads them to think you want them sexually. And the other is just by how you dress. Dressing sexy can tease them because how you dress tells others how to think about you. And the mere fact that you dress "sexy" says you are sexual. Even though I know that's not true, that's how it looks to everyone else. So if you want to stop being called a tease, then you've got to simmer down on the sexual innuendo. No more flirting as if you're a sexual girl, and no more dressing like one. It's time for an image makeover. Get into your closet and your vocabulary and get rid of everything that hints at your sexuality. In other words, lose the low-cut tops, tight pants, short minis, belly button ring, tongue ring—anything that would suggest you are ready for sex. I could go on and on about this subject. It's really an important one to get ahold of. So check out *Sexy Girls: How Hot Is Too Hot?* for more info. It will help you do a tease makeover and should get rid of all those catcalls and jeers from the guys you meet.

Hayley

Do Guys Think You're

HoT?

More about How Hot Is Too Hot.

Trust me when I say this: guys are visual creatures. They are turned on by what they see. You show them a bit of your boob or some of that long leg of yours and *bam!*— Testosterone City! They are instantly dreaming of what they saw. It might seem gross, juvenile, or impossible that a guy would want to touch your breast just because he can see a part of it, but trust me, it's true. I've talked to hundreds of guys about girls, and it's the same in whatever state, country, or province I'm in. They are turned on by your flesh.

We are so used to our flesh that we don't think anything about it. We undress in front of each other, we share a dressing room, we sleep together in our T-shirts, and we think nothing of sexual stuff. And so it can seem so strange to us that guys see a little flesh and they go all sexual on us, but it's true. That's why guys are more likely to *not* share a bed with another guy, king size or not, when crashing at a friend's house or on a road trip. *Way too visual for them.* They aren't casual about our bodies like we are. Any hint of flesh they see and it's daydream city, for better or for worse.

So if you are showing the very tippy-top of your cleavage because you think, *Who cares, it's not like they can see my breasts,* funny thing—no, they don't actually see your breasts, but they do start to imagine what they look like. Their minds start to wander down lower and lower. So show them a whole lot of cleavage and suddenly they're salivating over your entire chest.

They can't help but create a mental image of what the rest of you looks like. (Well, they *can* help it, but it's really, really hard. It's instinct, this stuff.) It's the same with your waistline. When you wear your pants down really low on your hips so that your skin shows below your shirt, they are imagining what's down lower. Show them your cute underwear, and it's all over. They're already salivating as if you're wearing nothing from the waist down. This is no joke. Guys' eyes see more than you show them. So the less you are showing, the less they will imagine.

I don't know about you, but I don't like the idea of any ol' guy walking down the hall thinking all fantasy-like on my body and imagining us doing things together. It's kinda gross. Sure, you might feel good about your target guy drooling you up, but he's not the only one in the hall with testosterone, is he? And besides, the Bible makes it pretty clear that causing someone else to stumble (i.e., to fantasize about you) is not cool with God:

> Be careful, however, that the exercise of your freedom does not become a stumbling block to the weak.
>
> 1 Corinthians 8:9

But I say to you that everyone who looks at a woman with lust for her has already committed adultery with her in his heart.

> Matthew 5:28 NASB

It is better not to eat meat or drink wine *or to do anything else* that will cause your brother to fall.

> Romans 14:21, *emphasis added*

Now that you know that your aggressive exposure of your fleshly parts is a stumbling block to the guys around you, what excuse do you have for flaunting your girly parts? It's really crucial to get this. It's a huge part of your image. Are you claiming to be a believer? Do you worship God, talk about prayer and your relationship to Christ, and then tempt every guy who comes across your path? If we want to develop the perfect image for you, we really have to figure out what that image should be, according to your faith, and then how to achieve it. So this chapter has just been an exercise in understanding the male part of the species that populates this planet with us so that you can better portray the girl that God has designed you to be.

Excerpted from *Sexy Girls: How Hot Is Too Hot?*

"Be careful, however, that the exercise of your freedom does not become a stumbling block to the weak."
1 Cor. 8:9

my dad is
driving me crazy!

Dear Hayley,

My dad won't leave me alone. I don't mean in a bad way like he's mad all the time, but he just is always around. Always asking me questions, always wanting to do things with me. It's like I'm his best friend or something. I love him and all; I just need my space. I mean, I have a life. What do I do? My dad is driving me crazy!

Larissa

Dear Larissa,

First let me just say, that's a good problem to have. Lots of girls would love to have a dad who gave them any attention at all. So take heart; it sounds like you have a great dad. But I totally understand about the "enough is enough" thing. Your dad needs to understand that you aren't his little girl anymore. You are becoming your own person, a young adult who has friends and a life separate from his. And it might just be that he's realizing that and it's scaring him. He doesn't want to lose his little girl. The best thing to do with parents like this is to talk to them. Let them know how you feel, and most of all assure them that you won't leave them forever. Tell them that you'll always be their little girl, just not in the same way as you used to be. You need them to let you go a little so that you can grow up, test your wings, and learn to fly. Help them to understand that being out on your own more now is just preparing you for when you one day will go off in the real world on your own. I mean, you can't stay home forever.

Encourage your dad by letting him know how much you love him. Plan times when just you and he can still go out and do stuff alone, but be honest with him and make sure he understands you don't hate him—you are just growing up.

Hayley

i feel guilty
when i say
NO

Dear Hayley,

I am on the leadership team at my church, and I am there three nights a week. I love helping out and doing things for my group, but sometimes when they ask me to do stuff, I'm just too tired or I can't get away from stuff at home. But I feel guilty when I say no, because I'm supposed to serve others, right? Am I sinning when I don't do things for my church group?

Adrienne

Dear Adrienne,

The short answer to that is no, you are not sinning when you don't do things for your church group. If you never did anything and refused to lift a finger to help people who asked, then maybe we might be able to consider some sin involved, but the fact that you are at church three nights a week says you aren't rejecting service to others. In fact, you might want to watch out for the opposite problem. Don't let your serving others become your main focus, your obsession. Because anything that becomes an obsession controls you. And anything that controls you is really an idol. If anything other than God is excessively preoccupying your mind, then you've crossed over into idolatry—even if that thing is serving in your church. Lots of people can become so obsessed with serving that they are no longer thinking of God but are thinking merely of what they can *do* next. Think about this: even Jesus, while he walked this earth, didn't serve 24/7. He said no by walking away from the crowds and getting alone with God and his disciples. Other things in your life are required of you too, like family, friends, quiet time, and studying, and you can't let one area of your life dominate the others, or you'll be out of whack.

I know from experience that the guilt can also come from the fact that you think nothing will or can get done without you. That you have to do it because you can do it best. But beware those thoughts. You are not God and not the only one who can do things. So allow others to step up and go into action, even if you know you can do it better.

All this to say, don't feel guilty when you say no. You have a right and a responsibility to say no occasionally. After all, if you wear yourself out by always being the go-to person, you will never have time for rest and recuperation. *Balance* is the word for you. Determine the best amount of time for you to serve, and stick with or near that amount as best you can. Then don't feel guilty when you say no to time that is over that amount.

Hayley

what makes a good girlfriend?

The Best Girlfriend on Earth

Is there such a thing? Well, there might be if she looks something like this:

She appreciates the things he does and tells him so.

She doesn't complain.

She's happy.

She doesn't tell him all her problems all the time.

She doesn't ask him what he's feeling.

She lets him have his own interests, whether she likes them or not.

She lets him have guy time.

She doesn't smother him or act too needy.

She lets him take the lead in things.

Excerpted from *The Dirt on Dating*

Dear Hayley,

I don't have a mom, so I don't have anyone to teach me about girl stuff. So I need your help. I have been dating this boy for two weeks. I really like him and don't want to mess it up like I did my last relationship. But I don't know who to talk to about it. What did I do wrong before? What do guys look for in a girl-friend? How can I be a good girlfriend?

Misha

Dear Misha,

When it comes to boys, they all have different ideas of the perfect girlfriend, but here are some things you can think about. I believe most guys appreciate a girl with confidence. And that just means that she isn't always worried he's looking at someone else. She isn't clingy or overly jealous. Confident girls have their own life; they don't get all lost in a guy and make him their everything. They are friendly to everyone, even strangers. They don't complain all the time. They are happy most of the time and appreciative of him. Guys like a girl who likes them, but not more than life itself. They love a girl who lets them be a guy and have guy time with their friends without getting jealous. Most guys want a girl who has her own life and isn't super needy but still needs him for the small things like lifting heavy objects, fixing a flat tire, or figuring out electronics. Guys like to be needed but not be all you need.

Being a great girlfriend really means understanding the guy you like and doing what you can to be who you are and become who you want to be, all while caring about who he is and what he wants. It's never easy caring for another person like that; it takes work both for them and for yourself. You can't get carried away thinking about them, and you can't get carried away thinking about you. It's a delicate balance of holding on and letting go. I don't expect you to get it all right or all wrong. And either way, you'll be okay. Think of this as practice time. Learn how to be who you are and then how to be the best girlfriend on earth. And don't get down on yourself if you fail. You will have plenty more opportunity to practice.

Hayley

friendless
i don't have anyone to talk to

Dear Hayley,

I started at my school two months ago and I hate it. I'm so lonely. I have no friends, and I don't have anyone to talk to. It's like hell. I hate my life and don't want to do anything but sleep. My mom says I need to get over it, but how can you live without someone just to talk to?

Becca

Dear Becca,

Friends are awesome. It's definitely great to have ones you can call on, but your mom is right: you can't let yourself get all bummed out, because it's only been two months. Give yourself a break. It takes time to get to know people and to let them get to know you. If making a friend is something you want to do, you can't just give up on it and sleep your life away. You have to put some effort into it. The main thing to do is to be really nice. There's no time to be shy. You have to make yourself talk to strangers, smile at people, and go out and do things. Girls need to see that you are nice to be around and happy. No one wants to hang out with a depressed girl. So yep, you have to get over it. Change your perspective. It's no wonder you don't have any friends after only two months at your school. You're normal.

In the meantime, before you find a new bff, I want you to turn your heart and mind upward.

Maybe God is using this time of isolation as a call to you. He's calling you to get down on your knees and go to him. Get into your Bible and read about him and his truth. Study it and memorize it. Let him know how much you need him. Close your eyes and imagine crawling up on his lap and telling him everything you want to talk about. He's sure to listen. But just like with your friends, you have to be willing to do some listening too. So take some time each day to do that. Find a great place in nature and think about how cool he is for making the things he's made. Make a list of stuff you're thankful for and read it often. Listen to worship music and let your pent-up feelings flow. God is there for you, and he is always willing to listen. And take heart—it won't be long before you'll have friends at school and life will be all rosy again.

Hayley

my dad says i'm addicted
to my
cell phone

Need I say more?
Help me keep it,
Hayley!
                    Jenny

Dear Jenny,

Well, all I can say is that you're not alone. Cell phone addiction might be one of the biggest addictions of this century. People the world over can't let go of their mobile. Lots of people have multiple phones, Sidekicks, and CrackBerries and talk or text on them for hours a day. Here's how to find out if you are addicted.

Are You Addicted to Your Cell Phone?
1. Do you spend more than 30 minutes a day on your cell?
2. Do you use it more than you mean to?
3. Does it freak you out to think of losing it?
4. Do you miss out on class or family functions because you are talking on it?

If you answered yes to any of these, then you are addicted.

Maybe your dad's onto something. But who cares, right? What's the big deal about a cell phone addiction? It is a big deal, actually, because an addiction is something that controls you. When you are addicted to something, you have essentially made that something your god. And that means that the real God has been demoted. Not only do you demote and disrespect God with your addiction but you disrespect people as well. Addiction to a cell phone, like to anything else, can cause you to hurt those around you. If your dad says you are addicted, then he's one of those who is feeling the sting of your addiction. Your family is more than likely becoming less and less a part of your life as your friends and your cell take up more and more of your mind-space. You may or may not have an addiction, but either way, it sounds like you have a problem. Your cell and your dad aren't getting along. So if you really think you want to keep your phone, then you have to manage your addiction. That means you have to take charge of it and make some changes. Your prescription for cell phone reduction follows. I know it seems impossible, but if you can't do it, then you should lose your cell phone!

Hayley

THE CELL PHONE ADDICTION CHALLENGE: CAN YOU DO IT?

- Never have a conversation longer than 5 minutes.
- Don't use your cell more than a half hour per day.
- Don't talk on it while you're walking to class. Be open to having conversations with the people right in front of you!
- Turn it off except when you really need it or your parents might need to get in touch with you.
- Don't carry it on your belt or hold it in your hand while you walk around the mall or at the gym.
- Don't look at it every time it rings if you're in a deep conversation with someone else, especially an authority figure or someone who is hurting.
- Don't have it on during mealtimes. Show the people you are eating with that they are important to you.
- Don't interrupt conversations with your friends to answer the phone unless it's your parents or another important person—i.e., not just another friend who wants to chat. Interrupting is rude and shows everyone that your phone is your idol. And being rude is caring more for yourself than others. That's the opposite of dying to self.

*For more on addiction, check out "What Is Idolatry?" on page 74.

- Never talk on it in a restaurant, in a class, or in the library. It's rude.
- Make talking in person more important than texting or talking on the phone.
- Manage your minutes—never go over! Going over means you are a slave to your phone. It has become your master, and as God's Word says, you can't serve two masters (see Luke 16:13). Choose God, not the cell phone.
- You only need one cell phone. If you have more than one, you are a glutton!

SHOP WISELY

modesty never looked so good

i keep confessing, but i never feel forgiven

"God is able to forgive anything that you confess if you're willing to repent."

Dear Hayley,

First of all, I just want to say that I just finished reading the book *Technical Virgin* and I couldn't put it down. It hit me so hard. I've been dating my boyfriend for almost two years now, and every once in a while we fool around. We're at the point now where we have sex almost every time we see each other. I know deep down that he is a good guy, but we just always end up getting caught up. I think part of my problem is that each time I confess it, I never feel forgiven. Is there still a chance I'll be able to go to heaven?

Tamsin

Dear Tamsin,

Let me ask you a question: if I hit you on the shoulder and say "Sorry" but keep hitting you, apologizing after each punch, after how many punches are you going to be convinced that I'm not really that sorry? Probably after just two or three, right?

Well, luckily for you and me, God is able to forgive anything that you confess if you're willing to repent. And to repent means to turn away from that sin. Tell God you messed up and don't ever do it again, and you will be free. It's Jesus's death and resurrection that gets you to heaven, not how good you are. So thank him for that. It's amazing!

Since it's super hard to stop doing what you are doing, please talk to someone you trust about it and see if they will hold you accountable. Tell them everything you do with your bf when you are with him. That's totally embarrassing, but it helps to know you have to tell someone. Also, you and your bf can never be alone together again. You can't trust each other, and it's too dangerous. Do you need to break up with him? If he's not willing to show he can control himself, then absolutely. Remember, your relationship with God is far more important than any boy.

Hayley

but i like
being mean

"Just because something feels good doesn't mean it's right or acceptable."

Dear Hayley,

I read your book *Mean Girls* and I really liked it. The only problem is that after i read it, i realized that i am kind of a mean girl. I mean, i'm not really, really mean, but maybe a little. But here's the thing—i kind of like it. i mean, i do it 'cuz it's fun. Like talking about girls who aren't around and laughing about the stuff they do—it makes me feel good and it's fun for my friends too. So is it okay if i'm just kinda mean but not super mean?

K.C.

Dear K.C.,

I know exactly what you mean. It's fun to talk about people. It makes you feel good, and it helps you bond with friends. And the truth is that if you don't talk about people, then it can be kind of hard to find anything else to talk about. Newspaper publishers all over the world make millions of dollars telling stories about famous people because we as humans love, love, love to read about the lives of people more successful or more tragic than us. This isn't new. The Bible talked about it centuries ago. In Proverbs it says, *"The words of a gossip are like choice morsels; they go down to a man's inmost parts"* (Proverbs 18:8).

But just because something feels good doesn't mean it's right or acceptable. God makes it pretty clear that gossip is a sin. Gossip might feel good to you, but for the person being talked about, it can be painful. It hurts people when others laugh at them, poke fun at them, or hate them. And gossip usually always degrades to

that, doesn't it? The best policy is to think about how you would feel standing in front of Jesus as he replays all the things you've said about people, all while those people are standing beside you listening to what you said as well. If you can't say something kind and loving about someone, then beware, you've traveled into the land of gossip, and gossip is a small but dangerous knife that will ultimately cut you deep. So no matter how easy it is or how great it makes you feel, you have to stop. You have to walk away from those who gossip. And you have to choose the holy path. If you don't, your spirit will suffer.

Take a look at God's words on the subject:

Do not let any unwholesome talk come out of your mouths, but only what is helpful for building others up according to their needs, that it may benefit those who listen.

Ephesians 4:29

You, therefore, have no excuse, you who pass judgment on someone else, for at whatever point you judge the other, you are condemning yourself, because you who pass judgment do the same things.

Romans 2:1

Make it your ambition to lead a quiet life, to mind your own business and to work with your hands, just as we told you.

1 Thessalonians 4:11

When we put bits into the mouths of horses to make them obey us, we can turn the whole animal. Or take ships as an example. Although they are so large and are driven by strong winds, they are steered by a very small rudder wherever the pilot wants to go. Likewise the tongue is a small part of the body, but it makes great boasts. Consider what a great forest is set on fire by a small spark. The tongue also is a fire, a world of evil among the parts of the body. It corrupts the whole person, sets the whole course of his life on fire, and is itself set on fire by hell.

James 3:3–6

Without wood a fire goes out; without gossip a quarrel dies down.

Proverbs 26:20

A perverse man stirs up dissension, and a gossip separates close friends.

Proverbs 16:28

Keep these thoughts in mind next time you are tempted to gossip. Carry them around on pieces of paper in your pocket. And let your friends know that you are getting right with God and will no longer participate in the gossip chain. You've got to do it and you've got to do it now! Are you tough enough?

Hayley

"You, therefore, have no excuse, you who pass judgment on someone else, for at whatever point you judge the other, you are condemning yourself, because you who pass judgment do the same things."
Romans 2:1

Ask Hayley

i want to
show off
my new body

"It's really not that much to give up. It's just a little more fabric, that's all."

Dear Hayley,

This year I lost 35 pounds, and I feel great! I used to be so fat and was embarrassed of my body, but now I love it. I want to show off my new body by wearing tank tops and miniskirts and stuff, but my mom says no. What's wrong with being proud of what I've done and letting people see the new me?

Gretchen

Dear Gretchen,

Congratulations on the major weight loss. Nicely done. And I don't blame you for being proud of your hard work. You should feel good about yourself now, but keep in mind that just because you want to show off, that doesn't mean it's okay for you to make it hard for the guys around you to be pure. When guys see a hot body like yours, it's easy for them to start thinking sexual thoughts, and those thoughts are sinful. So you have to be careful about not leading guys to stumble because you want to brag about your new body. You can still wear cute sundresses and other stuff that's not too sexy so you can look cute; just watch out for the sexual areas like your chest, the small of your back, and your newly slimmed tummy. Putting such temptation in the face of guys who want to be faithful to God is just unfair and downright selfish. You can deny yourself here in order to help the guys around you stay pure. It's really not that much to give up. It's just a little more fabric, that's all.

Hayley

my parents are getting a
DIVORCE
—what can i do?

Dear Hayley,

My mom and dad told me last night that they are getting a divorce. I'm so scared. I don't understand why they are doing this. My dad gets mad at me a lot, and I wonder if that's why he is leaving. I didn't want this to happen and I am so mad, but what can I do? How can I let them do this to our family? What do you do when your parents get divorced?

Kylie

Dear Kylie,

It hurts like crazy when your parents do stupid things like get divorced. And I know from experience how much anger and pain you can feel. But the first thing you have to remember is that this is in no way your fault. I know it's hard to change your heart when it feels like this is happening because of you, but you have to try really hard to be super realistic at this point. The thing that helped me was to think about my parents as just being human. They aren't the amazing, godlike people I thought they were when I was a little kid—people who could do no wrong and knew everything in the world. Now that you are bigger, you know that just isn't true. They are human just like you and me, and they have hearts that break, tempers that flare, and minds of their own. They are not perfect, and when two imperfect people get together, things can easily fall apart. Your mom and dad shouldn't have chosen divorce as the answer to their problems, but they must have felt it was their only option. Divorce tears apart a family and hurts the kids more than the adults. But they aren't thinking about anything right now except stopping their own pain. So

you have to give them a break and see things from the perspective of two humans wanting to break up. If you've ever broken up with someone, you know how hard it is. Your parents just can't get along anymore, so they are doing what they think is best for everyone. Now your job is to keep it together by telling yourself the truth. And that truth is (1) it's not because of you, (2) they still love you and will always love you, (3) they are broken and fallen human beings who are not and never will be perfect, and (4) it will be hard to live apart, but you will survive.

Don't let yourself wallow in the pain you feel. Don't concentrate on how bad it is or how you'll never make it like this. You can't afford to think that way, and it's not going to help. Instead step back a bit, spend time with your Bible, talk with your parents about your feelings, and make sure they both know you love them and you won't divorce either of them by playing the blame game. Divorce is never easy, but baby doll, you will come through this, and if you keep focused on the truth, you will do just fine.

Hayley

6 Things You Should Know

1. It's not about you.

The first thing to convince yourself of is that this divorce is in no way about you. It's about a man and a woman breaking up. It's their relationship that has gone south. It's their problem, their stupidity, that's made them make the worst mistake of your life. Sure, it might seem like the best thing they could do for themselves. But for you it's disaster. I know. But it is something they are doing for themselves. So believe me when I tell you that it isn't about you.

The biggest thing that helped me get over my parents' divorce and get back to loving them both was realizing that they are only human. I used to think my dad was like Superman or something. He was my idol. I followed him around wherever he went. In my eyes he could do no wrong. So when he left, I felt like he was leaving me, although I didn't realize it right away. I knew it wasn't my fault, but I thought that if he loved me, no matter what happened with him and my mom, he would never leave me. But he left, so I must not have been special enough to make him stay, right? Wrong. That lie tormented my life for many years. If only I had been old enough to understand that it wasn't about me, things could have been so much better. I could have had a life with my dad.

> "Unforgiveness hurts only you. You might think it's the best way to get back at them, but it really does nothing to them at all."

2. Don't break up with either of them.

Once you can convince yourself that it isn't about you, you have to make a conscious effort not to break up with either of them. They are both still your parents, and both should be part of your life. That means you might have to make a major effort to stay connected to the one you don't live with. And sometimes that effort might seem one-sided, but don't give up. They need to know that you don't blame them and you still want a relationship with them. So call them when you can. Send an email, a card, a note, whatever. Just do what you can to stay in touch.

3. Forgive them.

This is a big one. But the thing to remember is this: When you won't forgive people, you allow the pain they inflicted on you to remain a gaping wound exposed to the elements. Unforgiveness hurts only you. You might think it's the best way to get back at them, but it really does nothing to them at all. When you forgive, you can heal. Forgiveness seals up your wound and makes you whole again. It's like this: Anyone you can't forgive, you can't stop thinking about. And when you can't stop thinking about them, you keep reliving the injury over and over in your mind. It might as well be happening to you again and again. Then you're never free from them. If you want to be free from the pain, you have to forgive them and get over it. Move on. That's the only way you can heal.

4. DON'T PICK SIDES.

I know that one parent probably looks the guiltiest, like they messed up more than the other, but looks can be deceiving. In relationships it always takes two. They each played a part in the biggest mistake of their lives. And if you try to pick sides, you only supersize their mistake. So in order to keep the drama to a minimum, you really have to try not to pick sides. You have to avoid the blame game. Don't tell the other one what the mad one said. Don't take the battle on yourself. In fact, do all you can to stay out of earshot of the slamfests. The less you hear, the happier you'll be.

5. LIFE ISN'T OVER.

You might feel like a monster truck has run up on your life and pinned it to the wall, but that doesn't have to be the case. Your life can go on—in fact, it

must. Keeping focused on your goals, your hopes, and your dreams can help keep your mind clear. Spend some time writing out your dreams. Think about what you want to

> "Getting over things sometimes means giving it up to God, trusting him that he'll work this junk out for you, and then getting on with your life."

do, where you want to go, and who you want to be. This divorce will be not the death of you but the birth of you, if you let it. Use the negative for good. Trials and tribulations, if accepted as something good, can only make you stronger. The most successful people in the world aren't people

who have had blessed lives but people who have lived through turmoil and destruction and come out the other side. So focus on your future, not the past, and let this stupid mess become a step toward the next big thing in your life.

6. TALK IT OUT.

The biggest and best way to work out anything in your life is on your knees. Spend time talking out your pain and anger with God. Whether you pray by your bed or spend time journaling, the more you do this, the more you'll be free from the stupid choices made for you by your parents.
You can also talk to someone like a counselor or pastor. Sometimes just telling another person how you feel can make you feel a whole heck of a lot better. Just make sure that you aren't using this as an excuse to wallow in your pain. Getting over things sometimes means giving it up to God, trusting him that he'll work this junk out for you, and then getting on with your life.

Excerpted from *Stupid Parents:*
Why They Just Don't Understand and How You Can Help

Hayley Helps:

I'm CUTTING

and My Mom Doesn't Know

Payton's Story

Payton (not her real name) and I met online. She is part of a network of anorexic girls who encourage each other to stay thin. We started an online conversation when she read one of my books and emailed me. Here's what she first wrote to me:

Hayley,

My sister died in 2004, and i miss her sooooo much...
one day we got into a big fight over something stupid,
and we ended up not talking for a while, and a few months
later, my dad tells me she died from drug overdose.
when he told me, i thought i was gonna die, i couldn't
breathe, i felt my heart break, everything was so loud,
i couldnt think. the day of the funeral was so hard, i
didnt go to the ceremony, i just stayed with the body,
and cried. That was the last time i really cried.... i
didnt want the funeral to end, it was the last time i
could see her, or talk to her. so, after that i started
cutting and starving myself. It was my bodies way of
crying, it helps me get over some stuff...

Also, I had to go to my grandma's funeral, and my
cousins dad....was really inappropriate with me...so i
was all hating guys for a long time,...THEN...the same
thing happened again...but with a different guy....and
this whole time, i have had this total bitterness toward
god...i lost my relationship with him completely, and
its eating me up inside cuz my mom doesnt know. and...
its hard to hide it....so anywho...i find out that my
dad, who i dont ever see or talk to anymore, could pass
at anytime...and even though im really mad at him, it
still scares me you know?? and im trying to deal with
all of this and more by myself, and i dont talk to anyone about cuz....well i dont know why i dont...but it
just starts to get really hard after a while.

Now, everything is wrong. i cant do it anymore. god
isnt helping. i cut really deep the other night, im
scared and angry. i tried to end it the other night but
nothing happened. i dont want to be here anymore.

                                             Payton

Wow—heavy stuff. I wrote back to Payton right away:

Payton,

Listen to me. I hope you know I care about you and I really want to help you make your life better. I'm not going to try to fix you, what I want to do is help YOU to gain control of your life and to get over your fear and anger. So if you are with me then let's talk.

First of all, let's just pretend like ending it all is off the table. If killing yourself weren't an option, what would you want your life to look like? What do you dream of? What do you want for your future? It's time to stop being the victim and start taking charge of your destiny. Only you have the power to do that. You have tried many ways to take control of your life, but they haven't worked. But believe me, there are powerful ways to really take charge. Think about this, if you keep on doing what you're doing you'll keep on getting what you've got. The question is, is that enough or do you want more?

I think you want more, so now's the time to get it. You have the power inside you to change your life, regardless of anyone else around you.

Lately you've been a victim not only of mean and stupid people but of yourself as well. You hurt and cut yourself hoping that will give you some kind of control or relief. But that's not working, is it? Being a victim is a sad thing. Victims suffer. Victims are depressed, scared, lonely, and angry. So we've got to work things out in your mind so that you stop being the victim. Victims are powerless. But the good news is you have control of your victimization. See, a person becomes a victim by what they *think* about their life, not by what happens to them. That's why two people can be abused by their dad and one can become Oprah Winfrey and the other can become a drug addict. We become victims by how we think about and treat ourselves. And victims don't win. The battle for your future, your happiness, and your soul rests in your mind. You can no longer believe that things that happen to you and around you control you, but that your mind and what you decide to think about controls your feelings. I know this sounds really weird, and hard, but it is actually a

lot easier than it sounds. And it's your hope. It will give you the relief you want.

The best way to stop being the victim is to take control of your thoughts. So let's start there. Let's decide how you want your life to look, to be, and then let's figure out if that's healthy and will make you happy, or not, and then how to do it. If you take life in small bites you can handle it better. We can work through things and figure out how to take charge. Do the things to get you where you want.

I know we can't sit down and talk together. And I can't give you a big hug. But I am here. And I am able to help you get what you want out of life. So if you are up for it just say the word, and we can talk back and forth about getting out of the rut you are in and into the glorious sunshine. Do you want a change? Do you want happiness, and a future? Because you can have it, my love, you really can. You can't let the world tear you down and break you. You can be unbreakable, powerful, and sure, or at least you soon can be. You can have your dreams.

You can find love, and peace. You just have to want it. The thoughts in your head might be telling you this is a crock and you can't trust me. But ask yourself this, have those thoughts been helping you lately or hurting you? Do you want a change? Or do you choose misery? I'm standing with you. I am on your side, and misery isn't. Let's walk on together. Let's take charge and let's get you healed. If you are ready then make a list of what you want your life to look like. The things you want. Then I'll help you get those things if those things are truly good things, because only good things should be your goal. Bad things will only yield bad feelings. It's like planting a garden. Plant corn seeds and get corn. Pumpkin seeds and you get pumpkins. Plant bad things and get bad stuff out of it. Plant good and voilá, you get good things. Okay, I need to shut up now and let you think. Write back soon. I'm thinking of you,

Hayley

The conversation between Payton and me went on for a couple of months.

Once I helped her to understand that asking for help wasn't a weakness, she agreed to go into rehab. We set her up with a great place, Remuda Ranch. And she went there for 2 months to get her head right and her life back on track. This was the opportunity of a lifetime. If she hadn't have taken it she might have killed herself.

Now we wait. We wait to see if she's strong enough to take back her life, and we pray. Please pray along with me that Payton will be free from the ties that bind her. Pray for her mind and her spirit. And pray for others like her. If you can relate to Payton, then stand with her in her desire to get well and tell somebody. Email me or talk to a pastor, counselor, or parent. But don't let your mind tell you that hiding it is somehow giving you power, because it's not. Dare to be strong and step out and take God's hand. You can do it! And you are not alone.

is it okay not to invite
my best friend?

Dear Hayley,
My family goes on vacation to Disneyland every year. It's a lot of fun, and all my brothers come home from college to go with us. I really love it. But this year my best friend asked if she could come too. She kinda likes one of my brothers, and I think she just wants to spend a week with him. I really like her, but I don't want to share my brothers with her. I don't get to see them much. Is it bad for me not to invite her? I mean, she is my bff.
Frankie

Dear Frankie,

No, it's not wrong for you not to invite her on your family vacation. Will she be mad? Probably, but she'll have to get over it. Talk to your parents and let them know the situation. Ask them if they agree that this is a family time and if you can tell your bff that they won't let you bring anyone. That way she won't be mad at you; she'll just be bummed that she can't come. Just because you're best friends with someone doesn't mean you have to do whatever they say. You have to do whatever is right. And if she is only coming to get with your brother, that's not cool. And even if she weren't, this is a *family* vacation, and you have a right to keep it that way. So don't sweat saying no. Of course, if your brother is into *her*, you might eventually end up having to deal with your brother inviting her. Ugh! And if your parents allow that, then that's another big can o' worms. But talk to your parents and see if they'll fall on the grenade for you on this one. I think they'll appreciate you putting family first.

Hayley

is **birth control**

okay for me?

Dear Hayley,

I'm 15 years old and have a boyfriend. I really love him and can't seem to control myself when I'm around him. I want to be on birth control just to be safe but my mom isn't sure it's okay. What can I tell her? Is birth control okay for me? What do you think?

Lizza

Dear Lizza,

Listen, I don't think this is a question about birth control, it's a question about self-control. If you are sitting there telling me you just can't control yourself when you are around your boyfriend, then it's time to stop being around him. If you believe the Bible and want to be a follower of Christ then you can no longer say, "I just can't control myself." That's rubbish. You can control yourself. You just have to control yourself when you *are* in control. In other words, when you aren't with him. Tell your parents you need help. Don't ask them for permission to be out of control. Agree never to be alone with your bf again and ask them to keep you accountable.

The next thing is that you need to ask them to buy you a copy of my book *Technical Virgin: How Far Is Too Far?* It's time to start taking your faith seriously. Are you in or are you out? I know it will be hard, but you've got to decide who you want to be. And remember, the majority of girls who end up pregnant end up alone, because the guys leave them as soon as they miss their period. If you really like this guy you can keep him longer by not fooling around with him.

Hayley

my boyfriend has changed

—what's he thinking?

Telltale Signs
That He's Just Not That Into You.

Sometimes guys want to hang out with you a lot but not necessarily date you. Figuring this out can be difficult unless you know the telltale clues:

Physicalness—If you have been on a few dates and there has been no hint of any kind of physical affection—touching your hair or your arm, offering you his arm as you walk, holding hands, etc.—then this might just be a friendship.

Sweet talk—If he never says anything sweet like "I love your eyes" or "You smell so good," then your relationship might not be *that* kind of a relationship.

His friends—If his friends all say things like "You guys are such great friends" or are talking about your guy's other relationships, that's kinda a no-brainer. You're just buds, period, the end.

The rumor mill—If rumor has it that your crush is seeing other people, then chances are you guys are just friends.

Excerpted from *The Dirt on Dating*

Dear Hayley,

My boyfriend has changed. He used to be so different. We were the best couple ever, but now it seems like we are just friends. I don't know what he is thinking. When I ask him, he says there's nothing wrong, but he seems so different and I don't like it. What is he thinking?

Angela

Dear Angela,

It sounds like he's lost interest. Guys aren't as emotional as girls and generally don't have highs and lows in their feelings. They usually stay pretty steady. So if he's changed a ton, then he might just be over you. Of course, if he's going through some rough stuff at home or at school, then that might be the only problem. But chances are he's moved on without letting you know about it. Guys want to be heroes, and breaking up with you wouldn't be very heroic, so lots of times they just check out and wait for you to get tired of them and do the breaking up. If it feels like he's just not into you anymore, then it might be time for you to take matters into your own hands and break up with him. If he fights you on it, then maybe something else is wrong and at least you'll have gotten him talking. But if he doesn't put up a fight, then you'll know it's time to let go.

Hayley

my mom is
embarrassing me

Dear Hayley,

Help! My mom is so embarrassing. She doesn't know when to stop. I love her, I really do, but she is trying so hard to be my best friend. She wants to go everywhere with me and my friends. She's always acting like she's a kid and talking all funny and trying to be all "hip." My friends laugh at her and it makes me feel bad, but I don't want her to hang out with us all the time. What can I do to get her to leave us alone?

Blair

Dear Blair,

First of all, let's just say that this is one of the better parental problems to have. At least you know she loves you. But that doesn't make it go away, so let's see if we can't fix the situation here. There are probably two things at play here. One is that your mom loves you and wants you to love her like a friend. And that's not terrible. But the second may be that your mom so desperately wants friends and wants to feel young again that she is using you and your friends to accomplish those things. And that's where things go wrong. Your mom isn't trying to embarrass you; she's just trying to fit in and feel accepted by "the cool people"—that would be you and your friends. It's really hard getting old, and some moms handle it better than others. The thing you have to do is take it easy on her. Don't get mad at her and yell at her and all that, because she won't understand

why you are rejecting her. But she does need to lay off. So you need to talk to her.

Share your feelings about her being with you all the time. Let her know that you love her but you are growing up and becoming your own person and you need time with your friends without her. Help her to transition from being with you all the time to leaving you alone by scheduling "Mom time" to do things like going to the mall and going out to eat, but make every effort to help her understand that those things aren't going to happen every day. You have to be able to have your own friends and do things without feeling like your mom is just one of the kids. You need her to be the mom, the adult. And that means she can't be part of your "group." This is such a hard topic to bring up with parents, so I would suggest picking up *Stupid Parents* and

Not-So-Stupid Parents and asking her if she would like to do a book study with you, just as a way of helping with the communication between you two. Let her know you don't think she's stupid, you just heard the books were good for kids to read with their parents. In *Not-So-Stupid Parents* she will find some insights into your problem that might just help her stop trying to be one of the kids and start being the parent.

Hayley

> "You have to be able to have your own friends and do things without feeling like your mom is just one of the kids. You need her to be the mom, the adult."

COULD it all just Be a Big misunderstanding?

Let's face it. You feel like your parents just don't understand. And you probably don't understand them either! All you want is some space, freedom and respect. It can be hard when you feel like you're from totally different planets. But fear not! There's hope. With a book for you and a book for them, find out how to stop arguing, start talking, and finally understand each other so everyone can get along before you leave the nest.

is writing poetry a sin if it's not about god?

Dear Hayley,

I'm in serious need of help now! I went to this Christian rally last week and they said we should only use our talents like dance and poetry to worship God. So I've been only using my poetry to write about God. I haven't been writing about the usual problems that have been going on in my life (i.e., mean girl problems). So I've been trying to talk to God about these problems. I used to write the confusion, angst, and all those feelings out in my poems, but now I'm not. Since I stopped writing my feelings down, I've been going crazy—seeing the girl makes me want to scream, and when I think about her, I get major headaches and stomachaches. Now here's my big question—can I write my feelings out even when it's not for worship? It's like I go crazy without writing my feelings, and when I have all this emotion inside, I can't write about God either. Help! What am I supposed to do? Can I use my gift to help myself? Would that still be considered Christian?

Tiffany

Dear Tiffany,

I can understand where the rally people were coming from: it's good to use your gifts for worship. But when it comes to journaling, I think of that as my way of talking to God. It's the best way for me to tell him what I'm thinking and to get my thoughts out, just like you do. But I also know that I've used my writing in some bad ways, like using it to rehash my anger and other bad emotions just so I can enjoy them, kinda like getting revenge but in writing. Not so good. So what I'd suggest is that you use your talent for writing to write your thoughts and feelings to God. Then spend time in your Bible studying his answers to your feelings. Get a concordance and look up the subjects you are having trouble with. Then write what you learn after your journaling/poetry.

Think of it like this: David was a great poet. He used his writing, the psalms, to get his feelings of misery out, but he also followed each rant up with hope and truth about God. If that's not a good use of your talents, I don't know what is.

Just use your talents in a way that always leads you back to Christ. Enjoy the gift God gave you and have fun with it, but keep it faithful.

Hayley

why do they hate me?

a shy girl's mean girl problem

Dear Hayley,

i have a mean girl problem—well i have several actually. no matter where i go girls are always mean to me. i mean, i'm super shy and i don't talk to them so why do they pick on me? i keep my distance and i don't get in anyone's way but no matter what school i'm at i'm always the one they pick on. Why do they hate me?

Beth

Dear Beth,

I know what it's like to be shy. Believe it or not, I'm naturally shy, and it has really been a problem. I had Mean Girls too, and I blame a lot of it on my shyness. They thought I didn't talk to them or hang out with them because I was stuck up. But that wasn't it at all; I was just scared of them. Being shy can be like a big target for Mean Girls. And even though it's not fair, it's how it is. There is a solution, however, but it means doing some changing. It's like this: You can't control other girls. You can try, but you will fail. The only person you can control is you. And if you don't like what you're getting in your life, then it's time to change things, and by things I mean you. Because if you keep doing what you're doing, you'll keep getting what you're getting. Not all girls will lay off you completely if you are less shy, but it should cut down on the majority of them. A person who is nice to others is much more likely to get nice back than a person who shuts out others. So if you are lonely and sick of feeling scared, then refuse to be shy. Be courageous and step out in love. Loving your neighbor is a command, even for shy girls. And loving those girls by stepping out of your shy shell will help you to slowly break out of the Mean Girl rut.

So say hi, be friendly, smile. Don't expect things to change overnight, but you can cut down on the mean brigade if you can do this. Check out "Conquering Your Shyness" for more info.

Some girls are mean for no reason other than that they enjoy it, and there is no way to stop them. But if lots of girls are mean to you everywhere you go, then maybe it's time to take a look inside and see what you might be doing to make them attack, and your shyness seems like the best place to start. You can do this. I know because I did it and am still doing it myself. It's hard every time I walk up to someone and say hi, but I do it, and believe it or not, bit by bit it's getting easier. You can do it too—I just know it!

Hayley

Conquering Your Shyness

Are you super shy and don't know how to change? Being shy can cause you all kinds of heartache, but what can be done about it? I mean, you were born that way, right? Maybe, but that shouldn't be a reason not to change. People are born with all kinds of disabilities and learn to overcome them in order to make life better for themselves. Being shy shouldn't be an option for a girl who wants to glorify God and serve him and others. Shyness simply means that you are too focused inward, and because of that inward focus, you are afraid of others. They threaten your feelings, your space, your very person. You have in essence made their opinions of you more important than God's opinion of you. See, God commands us to love others. And loving others means being able to talk to them, interact with them, and care for them. If you are too shy to do that, then you are disobeying God's law. Shyness is often confused with being stuck up. And how

do you think that looks to a nonbeliever who is watching you? Does it represent your God well? It's time to start to consider what your shyness is doing for you and what commands it is keeping you from obeying. Breaking your shyness will not kill you, I promise. It might feel like it, but I know from experience that stepping out in faith and obedience and talking to those girls and saying hi to strangers will always yield success. Even if they reject you, you have the success of following God's commands and doing what he asks in the face of fear. So if you are ready to deny yourself, take up your

cross, and follow God's Word, then here are a few simple things you can do to move in that direction. You can do this, and believe me, when you do, your life will be much better!

> "Shyness is often confused with being stuck up. And how do you think that looks to a nonbeliever who is watching you?"

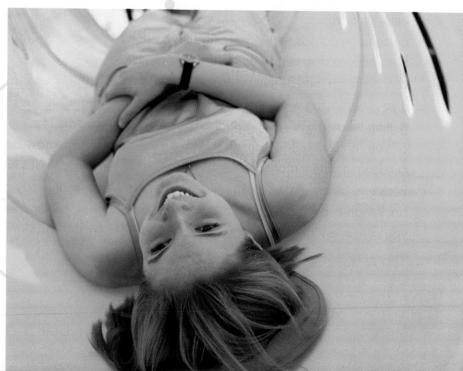

1. LOOK EVERYONE IN THE EYE WHEN YOU APPROACH THEM.

It won't kill you, even though I know it will feel like it. If you don't look into others' eyes, you can never love them.

2. SMILE.

Again, it won't kill you, but it might make you nauseous. You'll get over it, trust me. A smile is the best way to love on somebody. For some people it might be the only smile they get that day.

3. GO WHERE THE PEOPLE ARE.

Don't hide out. You were created to live in a community and to love others, not to be a hermit. That's hiding the love of God under a cup where no one can see it. He is more important than that. Don't worry about yourself; worry about him. Is he being seen in you, or are you hiding him from a world that desperately needs him?

4. GIVE PEOPLE A BREAK.

They are all hurting just as much as you, believe it or not. Pray for them. Care for them. Show them you love them by noticing they exist. You aren't doing this for attention or for affection; you are doing this for God (see Galatians 1:10). So don't worry if they still make fun of you and don't get you. It will take time for them to adjust to your change. They haven't learned what you've learned; they will need time to see you live it out over and over before they get the transformation. So don't fret.

> "Being shy shouldn't be an option for a girl who wants to glorify God and serve him and others."

i hate my job, but my dad won't let me quit

Dear Hayley,

I hate my job. I don't like the way my boss tells me what to do. He's so mean. This is my third job this year, and I hate having to switch again, but I just can't stand being treated the way I am. My dad says I have to keep the job, but that's stupid because I don't even want to go. How can I quit and still make my dad happy?

Julia

Dear Julia,

It sounds like you don't hate your job, you just hate being bossed. But unfortunately, that's what bosses do—they boss you—hence the name! Every job you'll ever have will have a boss who tells you what to do. They are always there, always wanting more, and always the boss. You can't expect them to always be kind and caring, because that isn't their job. Since this is your third job this year, it sounds like you have a problem working for people. The thing to learn is that if you want to have things, like a car, a house, CDs, clothes, and all that fun stuff, then eventually you're going to need to work for someone. Even if you never got another "job" but started your own business, you'd still be working for someone—your clients. And they can sometimes be bossier than a boss.

So take this opportunity to learn how to survive and thrive under authority. It can be really hard at first, but over time you'll build up your strength and you'll learn how to really do well with someone telling you what to do. Start with your dad. Let him be your first authority. And if he says stay at your job, then stay. The more you can learn to live under the authority of your parents, the better off and more successful you'll be in life. Successful people are those who have learned how to negotiate, charm, and work well with others. And you only get that through practice. So stick it out and learn the skills you'll need to become super successful. Then one day you can become the boss and be a better boss than all the ones you've had.

Hayley

what is
idolatry?

"I do not like to think of you as needing to have things pleasant around you when you have God within you. Surely He is enough to content any soul. If He is not enough here, how will it be in the future life when we have only Him Himself?"

—Hannah Whitall Smith

Dear Hayley,
What is idolatry?
I mean, isn't that
like making a
statue and wor-
shiping it instead
of God?

Katie

The Signs of Idolatry

If you are having problems with any of these, then you are in need of an inside look at your idols. For more check out *Idol Girls: What's Your Obsession?* Stop the idolatry and stop the pain.

Depression	Self-mutilation
Addiction	Hurriedness
Social isolation	Desperation
Loneliness	Violence
Financial loss	Guilt
Weight problems	Shame
Image problems	Fear
Anger	Worry
Bitterness	Discomfort
Envy	Broken heart
Hatred	Anguish
Never having enough	Self-hatred

Excerpted from *Idol Girls: What's Your Obsession?*

Dear Katie,

Let's get my friend Webster in here for a consult. According to Webster's dictionary, idolatry is "*immoderate [or excessive] attachment or devotion*" to something when that something is anything but God. In the Ten Commandments God tells us that we can have no other gods (i.e., idols): *"You shall have no other gods before me. Do not make for yourselves images of anything in heaven or on earth or in the water under the earth. Do not bow down to any idol or worship it, because I am the Lord your God and I tolerate no rivals!"* (Exodus 20:3–5 GNT). He requires that in order for him to be our God, he must be at the top of the list. If you have something else besides God that is all you think about, if you are obsessed with someone or something, then you have an idol. And the tragedy behind idolatry is twofold. One, it separates us from God, making us feel distant and unconnected. And two, it also affects our moods. If you are feeling depressed, isolated, angry, bitter, or any number of negative emotions, then you might just want to look into your life and see if you can find any idols—anything or anyone who you have elevated to the level of a god in your life and that controls your thoughts or your actions.

Hayley

Do You Have an *Idol?*

An idol is anything that is a rival to God. And a rival is anything or anyone who is in competition with or striving to be equal to God. Sounds simple enough. But again you say, "I have no idols, nothing that rivals God or I am attempting to make equal to him." Okay, I hear you, but let's still take a look at what a rival to God might look like in your life.

A rival to God would be in competition with him; therefore it would be something or someone who is fulfilling the same needs or job as God. Someone or something that serves us as well as God or that could meet our needs as well as or better than God, according to our puny little minds. That would mean a rival, or an idol, could be something or someone who might do any of the following:

Make you feel better

Give you approval

Meet all your needs

Relieve your distress

Give you hope

Tell you what to do to be happy

Demand your undying allegiance

Occupy all your thoughts

Forgive you

Save you

Rescue you

Protect you

Accept you

Heal you

Complete you

Condemn you

Can you think of anything or anyone who serves any of these needs for you? Someone you count on to meet all your needs or for approval? Is there someone you can't stop thinking about? Or who makes you feel bad about yourself? If you have anyone other than God filling any of these roles in your life, then you have made them a rival to God. An idol. And idolatry is a sin.

 Excerpted from *Idol Girls: What's Your Obsession?*

"Idolatry is your heart and mind's effort to protect yourself and to find meaning, purpose, and guidance in something other than God."

Dear Hayley,
Do people who commit suicide go to heaven?

A.J.

Dear A.J.,

That's a good question. Different people will give you different answers, but here's my take on it. First off, suicide isn't an accidental sin. If you kill yourself, you deliberately chose to defy God and tell him his commands are stupid. Deliberate sin is a rejecting of God (see Hebrews 10:26–29 and Numbers 15:30–31). Essentially you are saying that he isn't God of your life, you are. And people who deny God don't make it to heaven.

Of course, God does offer us forgiveness, so people sometimes talk about how even if you sin deliberately you can confess afterward and gain forgiveness (check out 1 John 1:9 to see how God asks us to confess our sins in order to get forgiveness). You mess up, you tell God you messed up, he forgives you, and it's all done.

The problem in this case is that after you commit suicide you can't ask forgiveness cuz you're dead. And don't think that you can just confess *before* you do it, because you can't be forgiven for something you are planning to do in the future. It doesn't work that way (Galatians 6:7-8; 1 John 2:3–6).

But supposing, and this is just supposing, that it's true that you do make it to heaven after denying God and deliberately disobeying him, what happens next? In heaven there will be ramifications for all who die with unconfessed sin. It's like this, not everything in heaven will be equal. Some people will have it better than others. Bigger mansion, better job, whatever. (See 1 Corinthians 3:10–15.) What's the big deal? Well, remember, heaven is forever! Ever and ever! That means that whatever you get there, you'd better love. People who live a life of holiness will have it better. Not that anyone will be miserable in heaven, but some will get better rewards.

Okay, since we're talking about suicide here, let's consider one more thing. Suicide is a completely selfish act. It not only kills you but also kills hope—hope for the others in your life and in your future. When I was 27, I felt like picking up a knife and ending it all, and what if I had? That would have meant I could never have helped the hundreds of thousands of girls who have read my books; that I would never have been able to answer your questions. That my husband would be alone and lonely, and my daughter would never have been born. My one act of selfishness would have annihilated not just my life but perhaps the lives and hearts of many others. So if you've thought about suicide, here's what I say to you:

I know you want to make a difference in this world, and you can't if you are gone. Thinking about that might just help you to push through the drama in your life. Find in you what others will need one day. Suicide is cruel to the many who God wants *you* to help. It says, "No one in the world matters but me and my pain." And that's why God hates it. Selfishness is not what he wants for his children. He wants us to be selfless, to die to our feelings of fear and self-loathing. He wants us to be free from the voices that plague us by being free from self-obsession. When you have thoughts of suicide you have to tell yourself that it's a lie, it won't make things better, only worse. You have what it takes to make it past this, believe me. You just have to get those negative thoughts out of your head and put some holy ones back in. Get into the Word, turn on some worship music immediately, and stop those thoughts. You can turn this around whenever you want to! Let the drama you're feeling now turn into something good in the future. Start making plans for how you help others make it through what you're facing now. You can do it with God's help. Just think: he put me here to answer this question. Stay strong!

Hayley

> "When you have thoughts of suicide you have to tell yourself that it's a lie, it won't make things better, only worse. You have what it takes to make it past this."

Life is full of struggles.

But a struggle with food doesn't have to be one of them.

If your life is controlled by an eating disorder, *we can help.*
Together, we can face the pain, conquer the fear;
together, we can give it all to God... *and set you free.*
Asking for help is hard; *living with an eating disorder is harder.*
Call Remuda Ranch at 1-800-445-1900 today.

Hope Healing Life

R E M U D A
Nourishment for Life *Ranch*
Christian Programs for Eating Disorders

1-800-445-1900 - remudaranch.com

my best friend is spreading rumors
about me

Dear Hayley,

My best friend is spreading rumors about me. She told everyone that I fooled around with this guy, but I really didn't. I don't know why she's doing this. It hurts really bad. She is in my youth group and everything, and she knows I don't do stuff like that, so why is she lying? How do I get her to stop?

Adeline

Dear Adeline,

Sometimes even best friends do really stupid stuff. Usually they have a reason. In other words, in their minds there is a good reason for saying what they're saying. Usually it has something to do with what they think you've said about them or to them. In other words, they are trying to get even. Unless your friend is just plain mean, I bet she has a reason in her mind for why she's doing it—not that any reason is a good reason for gossiping, especially about your best friend. Either way, I think it's time for a talk. Get her alone somewhere where she won't be embarrassed; that way she won't feel as much of a need to lie or be mean. Then tell her what you heard she said and how it hurt. Be kind, but ask her why she thought you were fooling around with that guy. Try not to accuse her of lying or gossip; just try to love her and ask her what she was thinking. If you can make it nonaggressive, you're more likely to get the truth from her. If you confront her and get all accusatory, she might lash out at you. Try to think of her as the friend she is who just made a mistake. It's always best to give friends the benefit of the doubt.

Finally, whatever she says, you'll have to be able to get over it. You might not like what you hear, but if she is sorry, then forgive her. Even though it still hurts. And if she's not sorry, then maybe she's not as good of a friend as you thought. You don't have to hate her, but you might have to stop being her best friend. If she is going to insist on lying about you and won't apologize for her mistake, then she's not a good friend. So have the tough conversation and put yourself in her shoes. You might be surprised what you find there.

Hayley

My Friend the Gossip Hound

What to Do When Your Friend Lives to Talk

The gossip seems totally fun to have around. She has all the hot G, and she loves to share it. Your bond gets deeper and deeper with each nasty little secret. But do you trust her? I mean, if you have a major trauma, do you go to her with it? Or do you know by now that there's no way she can be trusted? After all, she lives for good G. Does that include yours? A gossipy friend can spell disaster for you. First of all it means that nothing you say is safe. No matter what, if you tell her something, you can be sure everyone else will hear about it. And soon you find yourself censoring everything before you say it. The result is stress. When you can't relax with your friend, you aren't really with a friend. The second big deal about having a gossipy friend is that she feeds your tendency to want the juice. She leads you into places you know you really don't want to go. She feeds your appetite for other people's destruction. Gossip is a destroyer of people. The book of Proverbs says it, "*As surely as a wind from the north brings rain, so a gossiping tongue causes anger!*" (25:23 NLT).

With this girl you find yourself in one of two positions: either you clam up because you are afraid that she will blab all your stuff, or you dive into her flow and start craving more good stuff. Either way, is this a safe relationship or a toxic one? You have to ask yourself if your friend is a Mean Girl or a good friend. Are you supporting the enemy or the good guys? Whoever you are hanging out with, you are telling the rest of the world that you support that person and believe in them and who they are. You are saying that the kind of person they are is okay with you. So think about it: is that true?

How to Deal with the Gossip Hound

1 First of all, don't think of your friend as a lost cause. If she has no understanding of the meanness of gossip, then she has no reason to stop. So start to talk to her about it. Tell her what you think. Ask her what she thinks. Don't judge and condemn her; just talk about it openly. You gotta start talking it out, because that's the only real way to help others. You've gotta help her see that what she is doing is hurting other people.

2 "As iron sharpens iron, so one man sharpens another" (Proverbs 27:17). What do you think it feels like to be sharpened? Imagine having a sharp piece of metal rubbing against you, rubbing down the edges and sharpening up the corners. It's painful. And talking to your gossiping friend won't be painless either, for you or for her. But if you are called to be an honest friend, you have to start chatting and figuring out how you both can be more faithful to the truth that gossip is bad news.

3 Whatever you do, don't think that you have to gossip to keep her as a friend. What's more important, your spirit or keeping her happy? Choose today who you want to be and then stick to it. If you want to be more like Christ, then give up on the gossip. It might make her mad, but who would you rather tick off—your friend or God?

Excerpted from *Mean Girls: Facing Your Beauty Turned Beast*

is
kissing before
marriage
wrong?

Dear Hayley,
Is kissing wrong
if you aren't
married?
Brianna

Dear Brianna,

Wow, that's a good question and a really tricky one to answer. In *Technical Virgin* I said that even tickle fights and back rubs can be sexual foreplay, so you could easily say that kissing is much more so. Here's the deal: it depends on the person. Your thoughts and your hormones all affect how touching and kissing another person will make you feel. For most couples who like each other, kissing can be a real turn-on. Of course, it depends if you are having a heavy make-out session or giving a good-night peck on the front porch. You can see the difference.

The trouble comes with the guy, though. You can't know what his hormones are doing. You can't know how your lips are making him feel. Well, you can have an idea—if he likes you, then he's probably getting revved up. Listen, some people might tell you that kissing is always wrong before marriage, and lots will tell you that's not true. But neither have crystal clear biblical support for their claims; they only have interpretations and personal choice. You have to look at your situation, the butterflies in your stomach and the fireworks in your head, and make a godly decision. Is kissing your boyfriend or fiancé leading you or him to sin sexually in your thoughts? Does it make you want more action? Does it make you fantasize about sex? If so, then you've just crossed over to the "wrong" side of the tracks. Be honest with yourself and with your guy. And don't do anything that might lead you to think about each other lustfully. That's the test. Jesus calls this lust sin when he says, "But I say to you that everyone who looks at a woman with lust for her has already committed adultery with her in his heart" (Matthew 5:28 NASB). Don't go down that road! Do all you can to keep your guy and yourself from even thinking about doing things that are wrong.

Hayley

how old do you have to be to read
technical virgin?

Dear Hayley,

I saw your book Technical Virgin and I really want to get it, but my mom doesn't think I should be reading it cuz I'm 14. When am I old enough to read your book?

Tina

Dear Tina,

Why don't you ask your mom to get you *Sexy Girls: How Hot Is Too Hot* and to read it with you. Then after you guys have read that and talked about it you can move on to *Technical Virgin*. I think that 14 is a good age to read that book. You are learning all kinds of things about sex in school, on TV, and from your friends. So why not read about it from a biblical perspective? I think your mom would get that idea. Tell her you'll read it with her so you can talk about the stuff together and about how your circle of friends feels about the same issues. I'm glad that you want to find out about sex from a godly point of view. Lots of parents are scared to let their kids read books on sex because they think the kids are too young. They want to keep them away from the nasty stuff people do. Trouble is, unless you never leave home and never turn on the TV, you are seeing and hearing all kinds of nasty stuff all the time. It's time for us to have the hard conversations and get the real answers instead of burying our heads in the sand.

Hayley

why don't i feel bad when
i'm sinning?

Dear Hayley,

Why is it that when I sin, in the middle of it and in the end of it, I don't feel bad? My boyfriend and I know we aren't supposed to be having sex, and we don't want to sin, but we just keep ending up doing it. We talked about it and decided to stop, and we were good for an entire month. But since then, we've been going downhill Hayley, I don't understand! Last week I even wrote him this huge email and we both talked about it and cried for hours. I hate comparing my actions to the world and to the things we used to do. But tonight we had sex again and it seemed like it was "fine." But now as I'm writing this, the tears are streaming down my face. Hayley, I feel so hopeless and helpless. I know what's right from wrong, I've done every workbook and reading. . . . How do I stop messing up?

Dagny

Dear Dagny,

What you are feeling is what most of us feel when we sin. In fact, Paul talks about the same kind of thing: "I do not understand what I do. For what I want to do I do not do, but what I hate I do" (Romans 7:15). We do this because we are so sinful. But as Paul says, we can thank God that there is now no condemnation for those who are in Christ (Romans 8:1). That means there is forgiveness, but only for those who aren't deliberately choosing sin. It sounds like you two aren't strong enough to keep off each other, so it's time to get an accountability partner for each of you. Find a woman for you and a guy for him, and tell them each what you've done and what you want to avoid in the future. Then promise to call them at the end of each day you and your bf see each other and give your accountability partners a recap of what you did. When you know you have to tell someone about your sin, it's a lot harder to sin. Make sure these people are godly and will hold you to biblical standards. You and your boyfriend also may have to break things off for a time to see if you can be around each other without giving in sexually. It's time to call in some (in-person) help! Get on it, girl.

Hayley

my dad thinks i'm a
drama queen

Dear Hayley,

I have a problem with my dad. He just doesn't get it. I just broke up with my boyfriend, who I love very much. I've been feeling really bad and crying in my room a lot. My dad thinks I'm being stupid and that I'm just a drama queen all the time. He doesn't understand how bad I really feel. He thinks it's all just dumb teenage stuff and I should get over it. But I really hurt inside. Why doesn't he let me be and let me feel bad? I wouldn't tell him his feelings were stupid.

Kaili

Dear Kaili,

Ugh! Breaking up is the worst. I'm sorry that had to happen, and I know how awful it feels. The male gender doesn't always get girls and their emotions, and frankly it can freak them out a bit. That's why dads are often the ones telling you to get over it, 'cuz they don't like all the drama. Although I wish he would respect your pain, I can also see where he is coming from. He's lived a long time and he's seen things and felt things just like you are feeling. And he's learned that time makes it all better and that in the grand scheme of things, this isn't that bad. I know it seems like you wanna die, but he's right when he says you should get over it. Getting over it simply means not allowing this trauma to consume you. When you spend all your time focusing on or crying over a breakup, you end up making the pain worse. I think a good cry helps cleanse the wound, but if it's been two weeks and you're still wailing, then you've got to stop. Your dad might not know how to help you stop feeling bad, but I might be able to help you out.

First off, you have to stop thinking about your ex. That means get rid of all his pics, sweatshirts, love notes, and all the rest. Get rid of the stuff that reminds you of him. You don't have to throw it away if you can't just yet, but put it out of sight. Way out of sight. Put heartbreak in a box, tape it shut, put it under your bed, and leave it there.

Second, change your thoughts. Every time you start to think about him or talk about him or the breakup, say, "No. I'm not going there!" and talk about something good instead. It might seem impossible, but it's not. You and you alone have the power to control your mind. So use it.

Third, spend time outside. Do things. Get busy. Do stuff with your parents and your friends; just don't go where *he* is. Don't let that guy get you going again with all those emotions.

Finally, trust your dad. When he tells you to get over stuff, don't get all mad. Sit down and talk to him about how you feel. Ask him how to get over it. Ask him what he does to get over stuff. If you want to make your dad laugh, tell him that you'll get over the breakup if he buys you that cute convertible you've had your eye on! After he stops laughing, you can work down from there, but accept no less than lunch out together with him telling you some of his breakup stories from back in the day.

In other words, get going and get involved in a non-drama way with Daddy-O, and maybe you'll find out that getting over the guy isn't as hard as you thought it would be. Sometimes Father knows best!

6 Things Not to Do

When Your Parents Think You're Crazy for Feeling What You Feel

If you want to avoid an all-out fight over your feelings or just want them to stop with the lectures, then stay away from some surefire ways to just make things worse. That means:

Don't scream "You just don't understand!"
Don't try to *prove* to them that it's okay you feel the way you feel.
Don't tell them they are just too old to understand.
Don't try to hurt yourself to prove to them that you really *are* feeling what you say you're feeling.
Don't give them the silent treatment.
Don't argue with them over your right to feel.

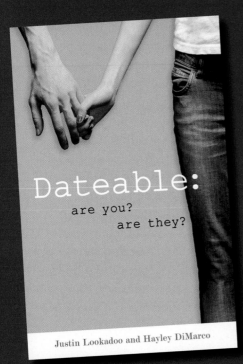

DRAMA QUEEN 101

1. THANK THEM.

Thank them for reminding you that "this too shall pass." Tell them you understand that you *will* get over it, even if you don't feel like it right now. Then explain to them that even though you know you'll be better, right now you just really need to feel bad. That will help you to get over it quicker. We each have our own way of dealing with things, and right now this is yours. So promise them that you will look on the bright side, remember that time heals everything, and believe that everything will be all right—after you've had a good cry or some time alone with your game console.

2. GET THEM TALKING.

This one might or might not work for you depending on your parents, but getting them talking about themselves can be a great way to get them off the subject of you and also to get them to remember how it felt to be a teenager. So ask them about the first time whatever it is that is happening to you happened to

them. Ask them what they did, what their parents told them, and so on. This might not be of any concern to you at all, but it does have a way of getting them to change the subject. A lot of times all parents really need

> "Remember that time heals everything, and believe that everything will be all right— after you've had a good cry or some time alone with your game console."

is to feel heard. They want to be validated—that is, told that they are right and you get it and thank God for them, that kind of thing. They need to feel needed. So even if you don't feel like needing them, give it a shot. It could take the heat off and might even help

you out with your situation. Best of all, it can remind them of their youth. And maybe through that they'll start to take your feelings more seriously.

3. WRITE THEM A LETTER.

If you have a hard time talking over your feelings with your parentals, then change things up and write them a letter. When someone takes the time to write something down nowadays, people have a tendency to pay more attention. You can sometimes express yourself better alone in your room with a pen and paper than you can face-to-face. So tell them your feelings and how it hurts that they don't accept that you have your own feelings, even if they do seem irrational to them. But remember, validating some of the things they've said to you in the past is a smart move. They might seem crazy to you right now or you just might believe them, but either way, you can calm your parents' frazzled fear that you're going off the deep end of emotion. Writing it all down can help clear

You know
you wanna
date me,
don'tcha?

Confused about
the opposite sex?

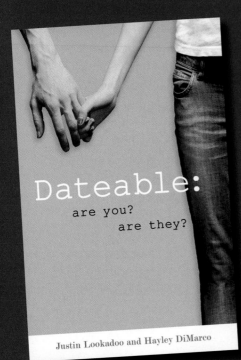

Dateable:
are you?
are they?

Justin Lookadoo and Hayley DiMarco

the
dateable
rules
a guide to the sexes

Justin Lookadoo and Hayley Morgan DiMarco

If you are now, you won't be once
you've read these bestselling
titles. Get the inside scoop on the
world of guys and girls in these
tell-all books. Don't try dating
without first being *Dateable*.

DRAMA QUEEN 101

1. THANK THEM.

Thank them for reminding you that "this too shall pass." Tell them you understand that you *will* get over it, even if you don't feel like it right now. Then explain to them that even though you know you'll be better, right now you just really need to feel bad. That will help you to get over it quicker. We each have our own way of dealing with things, and right now this is yours. So promise them that you will look on the bright side, remember that time heals everything, and believe that everything will be all right—after you've had a good cry or some time alone with your game console.

2. GET THEM TALKING.

This one might or might not work for you depending on your parents, but getting them talking about themselves can be a great way to get them off the subject of you and also to get them to remember how it felt to be a teenager. So ask them about the first time whatever it is that is happening to you happened to them. Ask them what they did, what their parents told them, and so on. This might not be of any concern to you at all, but it does have a way of getting them to change the subject. A lot of times all parents really need

> "Remember that time heals everything, and believe that everything will be all right— after you've had a good cry or some time alone with your game console."

is to feel heard. They want to be validated—that is, told that they are right and you get it and thank God for them, that kind of thing. They need to feel needed. So even if you don't feel like needing them, give it a shot. It could take the heat off and might even help

you out with your situation. Best of all, it can remind them of their youth. And maybe through that they'll start to take your feelings more seriously.

3. WRITE THEM A LETTER.

If you have a hard time talking over your feelings with your parentals, then change things up and write them a letter. When someone takes the time to write something down nowadays, people have a tendency to pay more attention. You can sometimes express yourself better alone in your room with a pen and paper than you can face-to-face. So tell them your feelings and how it hurts that they don't accept that you have your own feelings, even if they do seem irrational to them. But remember, validating some of the things they've said to you in the past is a smart move. They might seem crazy to you right now or you just might believe them, but either way, you can calm your parents' frazzled fear that you're going off the deep end of emotion. Writing it all down can help clear

4 Things to Do When It Feels Like Your Parents Are Discounting How You Feel

your mind and maybe even calm your nerves.

4. LEARN TO LAUGH.

One of the most important things in all of life is to not take yourself too seriously. If you don't want any hassles with your parents, then learn to take it easy on yourself. It might feel like the end of the world, or you might be feeling things you've never felt before—whatever it is that they are discounting, you have to practice laughing it off. This can help you in all areas of life, because from now on there will always be someone, somewhere, who won't validate your feelings. They'll think you've gone off the deep end or you're too emotional. Believe me, I know that of which I speak. Most of my life people have thought I'm a little out there emotionally. I'm passionate, and it can freak people out. But I had to learn to just get over worrying about what *they* think. I don't need others to validate how I feel . . . okay, maybe I do, but I've learned to find a few close friends who will sympathize with me and tell me I'm not crazy. As for the rest, I just expect them not to get me. So don't get all freaked out when your parents aren't getting you. Even though this might sound impossible, it is a goal worthy of your time and energy.

Excerpted from *Stupid Parents: Why They Just Don't Understand and How You Can Help*

"Ask them what *they* did, what their parents told them, and so on…. It can remind them of their youth. And maybe through that they'll start to take your feelings more seriously."

how do i stop
talking about people?

Dear Hayley,
Do you have any advice on how to stay quiet—like how to not participate in gossip and how to not reply to it? Thank you!
Alice

Dear Alice,

It just takes tons of discipline and practice. You have to promise yourself and your friends you won't do it anymore. Ask them to hold you accountable, and don't get mad when they point out that you're doing it. When people talk about others around me, I try to either walk away or say something totally nice about the person. That usually gets them all flustered. But if your friends gossip a ton, then you might just have to stop hanging out with them. Don't let their sin drag you down. Here's something to think about the next time you really, really want to gossip—'cuz I know it's like candy; your mouth starts to water and you just crave telling your friend that special something you heard about someone else. But try this: think about standing in heaven with everyone you know around you, and then picture Jesus going over everything you've ever said about them and telling them all your words. Think about how embarrassed you would feel with them and Jesus looking at you and knowing all the mean things you said. Whatever you do, make sure you pretend or imagine them hearing all you are saying. It can help you decide not to gossip. You can do it!

Hayley

will i ever be loved?

Finally, brothers, whatever is true, whatever is noble, whatever is right, whatever is pure, whatever is lovely, whatever is admirable—if anything is excellent or praiseworthy—think about such things.
—Philippians 4:8

Dear Hayley,

I'm 17 and I've never had a boyfriend. I feel like there must be something wrong with me and no one will ever love me. Why don't guys like me? Is there something wrong with me? Help!

Lacey

Dear Lacey,

Guys not being after you has nothing to do with *your* lovability. In the high school years most guys aren't really after love. They are having fun, dating, and learning about what kind of girls they like and don't like. They aren't ready for marriage and aren't usually looking for that girl who will take their name and carry their children. As you get older, guys will be looking more for "love-able" girls like you, and things will change.

So yes, you will be loved. Trust me. There is nothing wrong with not having a boyfriend. It can feel awful—believe me, I know—but it's not a sign that anything is wrong. It just means that the right guy hasn't come along. Rather than focusing on how miserable you are, why don't you focus on good things? Check out the things you love, the things that interest you, and put yourself into them fully. Focus on school, hobbies, family, and so on. One of the dangers of concentrating on your lack of love is that you start to appear miserable, angry, or bitter. And

that is *so* not attractive to guys. So you have to do all you can to do as the apostle Paul says: concentrate on things that are true and excellent and praiseworthy (see Philippians 4:8). Sometimes I think God uses our unmet needs as a way to test our obedience to his Word. If you can find your happiness in him rather than focusing on your lack of love from guys, then you are promised contentment and hope. You will find that your personality will brighten and your attractiveness will grow. God's Word is not only true but also useful for everything you need, including finding a guy. Do a study on contentment. Search God's Word for insight on how to be happy with just what you have and who you are, but also concentrate on how to make yourself better. As believers we are to be continually growing and getting better. So let's take your eyes off the world and put them onto heaven. And I promise you that your heart will heal and you will find all that you desire.

Hayley

i only have
guy friends
—what's wrong with me?

Dear Hayley,

I'm a girl, but I only have guy friends. Is that bad? I've tried to be friends with girls, but it's just so hard. They aren't very nice or even very fun to do things with. I don't get it. What's wrong with me? Is this normal?

Genna

Dear Genna,

Yes, it's normal, but no, it's not exactly a good thing. Some girls just get along better with guys. Guys usually aren't catty, and they don't gossip, cut you down, or try to steal your boyfriends. They seem like the perfect friends. But that's not the case. Girls need girls. We need people like us who really get us. We need sisters. And those of us who don't have them are missing out on something really special. And there are two special problems with having all guy friends. One is that girls with all guy friends are often seen as "just one of the guys." When that's the case, you'll find it really hard to get a date. Why? Because everyone thinks of you as a guy, not as a *Dateable* girl. The other problem is that if you do date and get a steady boyfriend, it's kinda hard to keep hanging out with all the guys anymore. Your bf won't want you with other guys all the time, and rightly so. So you end up losing your best friends. This is especially true once you get married. If all your friends are still guys when you get married, you'll be losing all your friends once you walk down the aisle, 'cuz a married woman can't still "hang out" with guys she's not married to. It's just not appropriate. So you need to find yourself some girlfriends. Don't be one of the guys anymore. Even though girls can be hard to be around, you've got to find one or two who get you. In the end you'll love it.

Hayley

Making Friends with Girls

What to Do When You Just Don't Get the Same Sex

If you just don't get girls and never have, or if you think guys are easier to get along with but you know you need girlfriends, or if you are just ready to make some true friends instead of mean friends, listen up!

I know how hard it is to be friends with girls. Believe me, it takes a lot of work. Guys are so much easier to hang out with. They aren't so emotional. They don't get so freaked out on ya, and they are just plain fun to be with. But that's no excuse to avoid girls altogether. And you might not believe me right now, but someday you're gonna need girls. God made us for communion with other girls. He didn't make it so that all our lives we would be surrounded by guys only. Certain things we can only get from other girls, and certain things

we should only *give* to other girls.

What you are doing by surrounding yourself with girls (and by that I mean have at least 3 good girlfriends) is preparing for your future. I know the future seems like a long way off, but it isn't, believe me. And if you can learn now how to be friends with girls, you will save yourself a lot of heartache in the future. Guys will come and go, but if you keep your friendships strong, you will always have a shoulder to cry on. And when you finally find "the one," your girlfriends will relieve a lot of the stress that you could put on him by being there to pick up the girl slack. See, guys don't need to know everything about us. When they do, they just get overwhelmed. It's too much to hear that your cramps

really hurt today and that you feel ugly because you don't have any new clothes. It's a bore to hear that you hate your hair or that your cat did the cutest thing today. Most guys can't handle all that we want to say, and that's why we need girls. So give the guy in your life a break and get some girlfriends.

But how do you be friends with girls? If you are anything like I was, you don't have a clue how to make friends with girls. So here are a few pointers to help you out. Remember, it's essential to have girlfriends, but more than 3 is overkill, because you won't have time to be good friends to that many girls, so none of them will be getting enough of your attention. So here are the things you need to know about finding girlfriends:

1. Effort

It's all about the effort. You have to be looking for them. You can't expect them to come to you and to do all the work. That's right, work! Making friends requires work, especially when it comes to girls. It might require that you call them a couple times a week just to talk, or in some cases just to listen. (Girls love to talk!) It might require that you ask them to do things with you. Don't wait for them to ask, even if you are shy. I realized a couple of years ago that I never asked girls to do anything because I was afraid of rejection. I had been rejected by girls for so long that I feared rejection even in adulthood, so I never approached any of them to do anything with me. When I realized what I was doing, I decided to get over it and get on with life, and I started asking them to lunch, to the movies, to dinner, and all kinds of things. Some of them said no, they were too busy, and I had to fight the fear of rejection, but I fought it and went on. Finally I found some who were really excited to be with me, and their answer was more often yes. I am so thankful that I gave it a shot and took the risk. I don't know where I'd be today without my dear friends.

2. Maintain the love

Girls usually need more attention than guys. I know that I could go an entire month without calling my guy friends, but once we talked again it would be like we had been together all month. They didn't hold a grudge against me for not calling. It's so great. But girls are just different. They kinda like to be kept in the loop. So here are some ideas to help them feel loved:

- send an e-card for no reason
- drop them a note in the mail
- call just to see how their day is going
- put a note in their locker saying "Hi"
- buy them a gift, like their favorite candy or magazine
- pick a flower and give it to them
- find a way to let them know you are thinking about them. Get creative. It doesn't take too much time or energy.

3. LEARN TO SPEAK GIRLESE

If you aren't used to being around girls, then a few pointers on how they communicate might help you out. Let's start with how guys talk for comparison. Guys usually communicate like a football game. The guy *telling* the story is on offense; the *listener* is on *defense*. At some point the guy on offense scores and kicks the ball off to the other team (guy), who then takes the ball and is off onto *his* story. Passing off and whose ball it is are clear. They always have a goal in mind—a point that one guy must get to so that the other guy can then take the ball. Getting to the point is crucial in guy world.

Girls, on the other hand, usually communicate like a game of Twister. We pick a subject and get to talking on it. An-other girl interrupts with a comment on the topic, and then it goes back to the first girl. Interruptions occur frequently and may take the story off of topic for a few minutes, but we get back on topic with a kind, "I'm sorry, I just had to say that. Now where were you?" The goal for girls often isn't anything more than just speaking—most of the time, we don't have to have a point. We don't have to find a fix for our problems or work anything out by the end of the conversation. We feel better if we can just tell another person about it. This freaks guys out! Guys want to get to an end, to have a point. That's why girl talk can be frustrating to guys. We don't need to figure anything out; we just need to dump and then we are all better. Guys don't dump, generally. They work things out alone in their head and save talking for something with a point. Their whole goal in a conversation is to get to the point, not to just talk with no end in sight.

If you are used to guy talk, hanging out with girls might be a little challenging to you. It was for me. Gab, gab, gab. But remember, with girls you can interrupt, change the subject, and make comments. It's girlese. Watch how they talk and start to notice their need to just blab. If you listen, you score, but if you blab some yourself, you score big too. Being able to just dump your emotions on someone who gets you is the most amazing feeling. And girls get that part of you better than any guy ever could.

Excerpted from *Mean Girls: Facing Your Beauty Turned Beast*

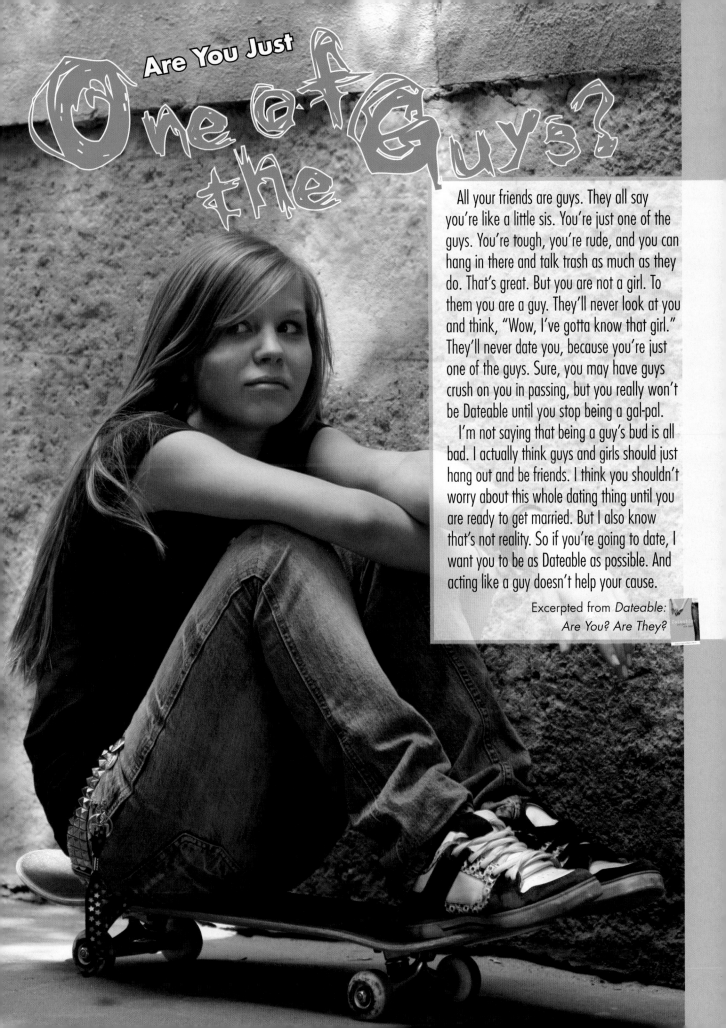

Are You Just One of the Guys?

All your friends are guys. They all say you're like a little sis. You're just one of the guys. You're tough, you're rude, and you can hang in there and talk trash as much as they do. That's great. But you are not a girl. To them you are a guy. They'll never look at you and think, "Wow, I've gotta know that girl." They'll never date you, because you're just one of the guys. Sure, you may have guys crush on you in passing, but you really won't be Dateable until you stop being a gal-pal.

I'm not saying that being a guy's bud is all bad. I actually think guys and girls should just hang out and be friends. I think you shouldn't worry about this whole dating thing until you are ready to get married. But I also know that's not reality. So if you're going to date, I want you to be as Dateable as possible. And acting like a guy doesn't help your cause.

Excerpted from *Dateable:*
Are You? Are They?

how do i
pick the right
college?

Dear Hayley,

I've applied to a few colleges and was accepted to all of them. I really like one of them a lot, but I'm not sure it's where God wants me to go. How do I choose? What if the one I want isn't the right choice? How do you know where God wants you to go?

Kerri

Dear Kerri,

Making big decisions like that can seem impossible. What if you choose wrong? How do you know? I know exactly what you mean, but here's the thing about choices: God leaves them up to you. As long as none of them are sinful choices, they are all up to you. If you aren't getting a clear gut feeling about God pushing you to one in particular, then it's up to you to choose. It's like this: think of your choices as a big playground. You can play on the monkey bars, or the swings, or the teeter totter, and God won't be mad about any of those choices. He doesn't care which you choose as long as you stay on the playground. It's called free will, and it allows you to set your own path. And the most amazing thing is that God promises to go down any path you choose with you, as long as it isn't a sinful choice. Like it says in Romans 8:28, God works all things together for the good of those who love him—even things like college choices.

So I say pick the one that sounds best to you. Whatever fits your major, location, or just overall feel of the campus and culture. Talk to your parents, talk to students, and do the research so you can make an informed choice, and then go with your gut. Then be happy with your choice and know God goes with you wherever you go. He can use you no matter where you go. Just keep alert, pray, and listen. You'll be just fine.

Hayley

how do i get my parents to let me do **what i want to do?**

Dear Hayley,

My parents are super overprotective. They won't let me do anything, and it's making me crazy. Like all my friends have cell phones, but I can't have one, because my parents say they are a distraction. And my friends have curfews that are way later than mine, so I can't do stuff with them, and I hate it. Why are my parents so strict? I don't want to do bad things, just normal stuff. How can I get them to let me do what I want?

Emi

Dear Emi,

It sounds like your parents aren't ready to let go, or maybe you've done something that broke their trust that you're not telling me about. More than likely they still see you as the little girl you once were and can't think of you as the adult who you are becoming. And believe me, that's normal and okay, but I know it can be really hard. They are doing their best to protect and care for you, and I doubt they are just trying to be mean. There are some things you can do when your parents are overprotective, though, to help them come to terms with your approaching adulthood.

First of all, you have to prove to them that you are just as protective of yourself as they are. That way they can trust you to make good decisions. Talk to them about what concerns them and tell them that you agree with them. In other words, share their concerns; don't discount them. When you agree with them, they will think you are more mature and being reasonable. Find ways

to compromise with them. See if you can't meet in the middle with stuff you want to do. Don't get all upset when they won't let you do just what you want, but think of each compromise they make as one more step toward getting what you want. You have to learn to negotiate. Give them what they want so you can get what you want. Let's call it the Art of the Deal. That means you learn about their concerns, agree with them, and then find something that can satisfy you both. Overprotective parents can be challenging, but if you are up for the challenge, they can teach you a ton about getting ahead in the real world. Have your parents check out *Not-So-Stupid Parents* in the bookstore. It has some good info on helping the overprotective parent loosen up a bit. And at the same time you can check out *Stupid Parents* to get more ideas about helping them to see that you can handle more responsibility.

Hayley

3 WAYS
to Show Overprotective Parents That
YOU CAN BE TRUSTED

1. DON'T HIDE THINGS FROM THEM.

If they feel like you are hiding stuff, then they are more likely to try to control your life in order to protect you. So don't be all secretive. Keep your door open. Invite them into your room to talk. Share stuff with them, like your favorite music or hobby or whatever is unique to you. Make them a part of your life, and they'll be less likely to worry about you because they'll feel they know you inside and out.

2. INTRODUCE THEM TO YOUR FRIENDS.

The more they get to know your friends, the more they can trust you with them. If you have friends they don't know, they might start to imagine all kinds of horrible things you guys are doing together. An informed parent is a more relaxed parent.

3. APOLOGIZE.

If you mess up and do something stupid or against the rules, apologize quickly. Agree with them that you were wrong and explain why you did what you did. Help them to understand that as you grow up, you will do more and more things independently, but they can trust you because you know the dangers out there and you know how to be careful.

"Make them a part of your life, and they'll be less likely to worry about you because they'll feel they know you inside and out."

They miss that warm, fuzzy feeling.

And it's cool. We know you do too. Sometimes. Maybe. Just a little.

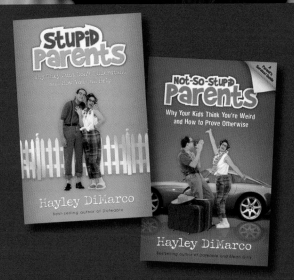

Mom used to be your hero and Dad could do no wrong; what happened?

Growing up brings a lot of challenges, including knowing how to get along with your parents. It can be hard when you feel like you're from totally different planets. But fear not! There's hope. With a book for you and a book for them, find out how to stop arguing, start talking, and finally understand each other so everyone can get along before you leave the nest.

Available at bookstores everywhere

www.hungryplanet.net

www.revellbooks.com

she started it, so can i
fight back?

"When a girl laughs at you, slanders you, or hates you, that's not permission for you to do any of the same."

where does the word
fornication
come from and what *exactly* does it mean?

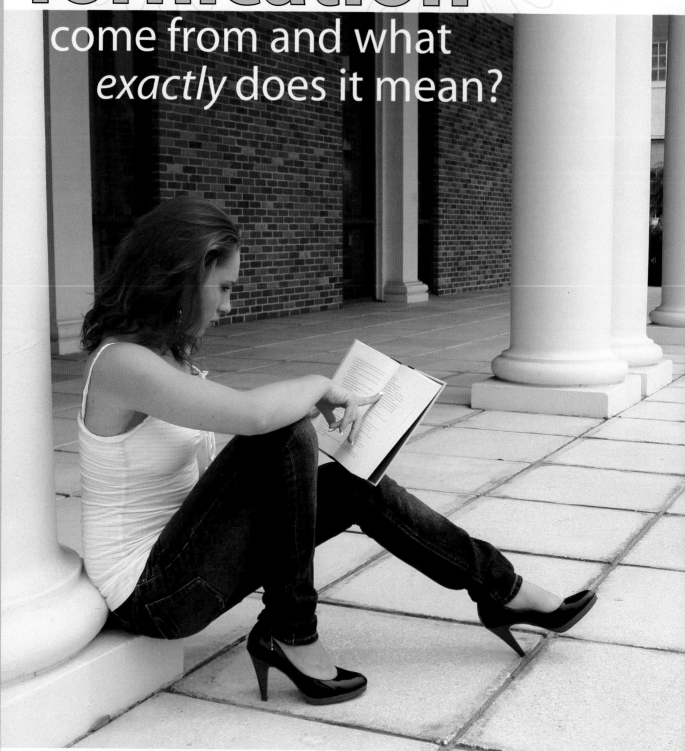

Dear Hayley,
I always hear pastors talking about "fornication," but I don't understand what it means, exactly. Is it just sex or what?
Paige

Dear Paige,

Fornication is defined as "consensual sexual intercourse between two persons not married to each other." But wait, there's more. To truly understand the word, you have to get the definition of sexual intercourse. Lots of people think that just means baby-making sex, but the truth is that intercourse is more than that. It's defined as "physical contact between individuals that involves the genitalia of at least one person."

So you don't have to have two naked people in order to have fornication. And fornication is a biblical term that is listed as a sin. That means that God commands us not to do it—probably why your pastor is talking about it. I'm not going to go into more detail here, but you might be interested in reading my book *Technical Virgin: How Far Is Too Far?* to shed more light on this touchy subject (pun intended).

Hayley

my parents
don't trust me
—what do i do?

Dear Hayley,

I did something really stupid and got in so much trouble, and now my parents don't trust me. They won't let me do anything anymore, and they watch me like a hawk. I'm not a bad person, I just messed up, but it seems like they've lost all faith in me. I want them to trust me—what can I do to make them?

Crystal

Dear Crystal,

Broken trust is one of the hardest things to repair, but if you are up for the challenge, it can be done. It is just going to take time and effort. But the payoff will be worth it. What you have to do is concentrate on being super consistent. From here on out, they are going to have to see a change, and they can best see that if you are consistently honest, open, and present. That means you have to check yourself and make sure that little white lies aren't the norm in your parental communication. Be super honest with them so they can see how trustworthy you are. You also have to be really open with them. Tell them everything you are doing and call them a lot when you are out of their sight.

Just help them to stay tuned with your life so they know it is going smoothly. Also, you have to be around. Don't run off and hide yourself; get involved at home. Help around the house, eat with them, watch TV with them. Be involved. The more they see you, the more they will start to trust you. Gaining back their trust will take time and effort, but you can do it. Just remember your goal and remember that everything you do has an effect on your future. Realize that the person who has broken trust *always* feels ready to move on sooner than the person whose trust was broken. Don't blame them for not trusting you; blame yourself for not being trustable. And get to changing that.

Hayley

how
HONEST
are you?

"Be honest with yourself about yourself."

Be honest with yourself about yourself. Seems like a no-brainer, but it's really not. If you can't be honest with yourself about yourself, then you can't be honest with anyone. And frankly, people who lie to themselves look like idiots. When you let yourself lie to yourself, you systematically destroy all your relationships, not just the one with your parents. Self-deception is a nasty thing. So get real and keep it real. This means that you take a long, hard look at who you are, how you treat others, and what you think about most often.

Who are you when no one is looking?
If you think you're a trustworthy, honest, and reliable person, does that hold up when you really look at yourself? Are you really all of those things? Or are you two different people when you are alone and when you are with someone else?

Are you really all that trustworthy?
You might get totally ticked when people don't trust you. But think about it—would *you* trust *you*? What's your true track record? Do you do what you say you'll do when you say you'll do it?

Why do you lie?
Sometimes you might lie to yourself out of self-protection. You think that if you don't

trust your parents, then you can't be hurt by them. But the truth is, when you think the worst of people, you are more likely to get the worst from people. You tend to get what you expect when it comes to others. Besides, think about how you feel when your parents don't trust you. They feel just as bad when you think *they* can't be trusted with your feelings. Their track record might not be the best, but you can help change that when you start to get honest with yourself.

Excerpted from *Stupid Parents*

CAN YOU BE TRUSTED?

A QUIZ

1 I've lied to my parents:
   a. never
   b. once
   c. a few times
   d. more than a few times

2 When I say I'm going to do something, I do it:
   a. right away
   b. within a few days
   c. whenever I can get to it

3 I think my parents hate me.
   True ☐   False ☐

4 I'm old enough to make my own decisions; I don't need my parents' advice.
   True ☐   False ☐

5 I'm always right.
   True ☐   False ☐

6 I don't need my parents. I can do life just fine on my own.
   True ☐   False ☐

7 I owe my parents a lot for all they've done for me.
   True ☐   False ☐

8 My parents **never** listen.
   True ☐   False ☐

Scoring
1. a = 3, b = 2, c = 1, d = 4
2. a = 1, b = 2, c = 3
3. True = 2, False = 1
4. True = 2, False = 1
5. True = 3, False = 1
6. True = 3, False = 1
7. True = 1, False = 2
8. True = 3, False = 1

13–22: Less than honest.
Bad news—you might not really be keeping it real. You have some really strong ideas that might be totally wrong. Try to look at life more honestly and dare to trust. Because if you can trust others to be honest, then you can start to be more honest with yourself.

8–12: Honesty is your policy.
Sounds like you're pretty straight up with yourself, but be careful of those little lies that you might tell yourself just to make yourself feel better. In the end, they only make you feel worse.

Excerpted from *Stupid Parents*

my boyfriend is **abusive**
but i can't leave him

"If you believe God's Word, then believe me when I say that the man God has planned for you will never hit you or slap you."

Dear Hayley,
I feel really stupid saying this, but here goes: my bf is abusive, but I can't leave him because I love him too much. I know he doesn't mean to hurt me, but sometimes I do stupid stuff and he just gets too angry and slaps me. It's not like he hits me or anything; he just can't always control himself. I love him and want to help him be a better person, so what can I do to help him?

Deirdre

Dear Deirdre,

Love can forgive many, many things, it's true. And we should help one another to be better people. But this might come as a shock: if your boyfriend is hurting you, then the best way to love him and help him is to break up with him. See, when you stay with him, you are only being selfish. You are sticking with him in order to fix him, because fixing him would make you happy and complete. But the truth is, you can't fix him. You cannot change him; only he can change himself, and until he loses enough people, he's not going to change. Girls who stick with guys who abuse them are lying to themselves. And that means that as long as you live the lie, you will never find peace, joy, or love. Here are 7 lies you might be believing:

He doesn't mean to do it.
He loves me, he really does.
He wants to stop.
I deserve it.
I can't live without him.
If I lose him, I'll never find love again.
Love is supposed to hurt.

If you believe any of these, then you are lying to yourself. The healthiest and most successful and confident girl is not the girl who puts up with abuse but the girl who chooses truth over lies. Lies never end well, so it's time to walk away from this guy and pick up the pieces. You can no longer bow down to his whims. This guy, this human, has become more powerful than God in your life. He runs your life; he tells you what to do and when. He has taken your focus off the true God and made you an idol worshiper. Just like the wooden and gold idols of biblical days, this idol will bring you nothing but destruction. God warns us against setting up these false idols, so please take heed.

Ask yourself, *"Am I now trying to win the approval of men, or of God? Or am I trying to please men? If I were still trying to please men, I would not be a servant of Christ"* (Galatians 1:10). Think about it, because those who practice idolatry by loving man more than God will find themselves locked out of heaven, according to Revelation 22:15: "Outside are the dogs, those who practice magic arts, the sexually immoral, the murderers, <u>the idolaters</u> and everyone who loves and practices falsehood." More is at stake here than romance—your spirit is at stake. So don't be deceived by his momentary kindness and affection. A guy who truly loves you will never hit you. If a guy does hit you, then he has shown that he has not chosen you as his love.

You have to know that God's plan for your life is for you to have a man who loves you the way Christ loves you and even died for you. His Word makes it clear when he talks about man and wife. And that is the ultimate goal of dating/marriage. If you believe God's Word, then believe me when I say that the man God has planned for you will never hit you or slap you. He will only do what's best for you. You have to trust God with more than your salvation; you have to trust him with your heart. Breaking up will be hard, but in that trial you will truly come face-to-face with your God if you are willing to trust him. Check out *The Blessings of Brokenness* by Charles Stanley and my books *The Dirt on Breaking Up* and *The Art of Rejection*. Between those three, you should have all you need to do what you have to do. My prayers are with you, dear one.

Hayley

For more help with an abusive relationship check out these websites. There are people to talk to and places you can go to get some answers.
http://www.loveisrespect.org/
http://www.ndvh.org/

Basic instructions for the heartbroken *and* the heartbreaker.

A Dateable Book

The *Dirt* on
Breaking Up

Hayley DiMarco & Justin Lookadoo

The *Dirt* on
Dating

Hayley DiMarco

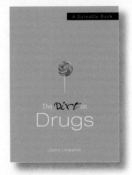

The *Dirt* on
Drugs

Justin Lookadoo

The *Dirt* on
Sex

Justin Lookadoo

It's real. It's raw. It's true. It's the Dirt.

i'm so depressed because
i never get what i want

Dear Hayley,

I'm having a lot of problems with being depressed. i can't even get out of bed sometimes because i'm so depressed. It's just that my life is miserable. My parents can't afford anything, so i never get anything i want. All my friends have nice clothes and cars and stuff, and i have nothing. My mom drives me to school and my clothes used to be my sister's. Ugh! I hate my life. How can i be happy when i'm so poor?

Leanne

Dear Leanne,

I know how hard it is to want stuff you can't have, especially when your friends seem to get everything they want. But you are missing out on something beautiful. You have a chance in front of you that not a lot of people have, and that is a chance for real joy and peace. See, when you feel depressed, it's because you think you deserve something that you aren't getting. Your whole focus is on that thing or person. You tell yourself, "If I could only have this or that, then I would be happy." But that's not the truth. Happiness has nothing to do with things. Sure, your friends might be excited to get new stuff and they might be happy for a few hours or a day, but the truth is, they aren't always happy either, 'cuz stuff can't bring lasting happiness. And here's where you're in a good position to change how you feel. You see, depression is just misplaced longing—longing for the wrong thing. The Bible tells us that God is the source of our happiness. He's the only one to truly make you feel whole and happy. But even if you love him, you aren't going to find happiness until you love him more than you love the stuff you want. My dear friend, you have made stuff your idol. You treat it like a god whose "soul" job is to make you happy. You believe that if you can attain that god (the stuff), all your problems will be solved. That's not only wrong, it's a sin.

Depression can be an awful thing. Your mind hurts, your emotions hurt, and even your body hurts, but it all stems from your thoughts. What do you allow yourself to think about? The truly happy person doesn't focus on what they lack but focuses on what they have. Depression like yours is under your control. You simply need to change your focus. Make a list of everything you *do* have. Things like a bed, a roof, food, a family. Many people around the world don't have those things. When you compare yourself to them, you are very wealthy. I guarantee you that if you can make your goal seeking God, you will find happiness. That's where you have it so good. The reason the Bible says it's harder for a rich man to get to heaven than it is to get a camel through the eye of a needle (see Matthew 19:24) is because your friends who get all they want don't get the chance to have nothing but God. They don't often get the chance to say to him, "You're all I need" and mean it. Yep, being poor and having little is a blessing in disguise. Check out his Word and see if knowing these things doesn't make you feel better:

Romans 15:13
James 1:2
Luke 6:24
1 Timothy 6:9
Psalm 37:4

Your best life isn't intended to be in the here and now; it's waiting for you in heaven. So keep focused on the goal, and trust God to give you all that you desire as your desires become more and more holy.

Hayley

"The Bible tells us that God is the source of our happiness. He's the only one to truly make you feel whole and happy. But even if you love him, you aren't going to find happiness until you love him more than you love the stuff you want."

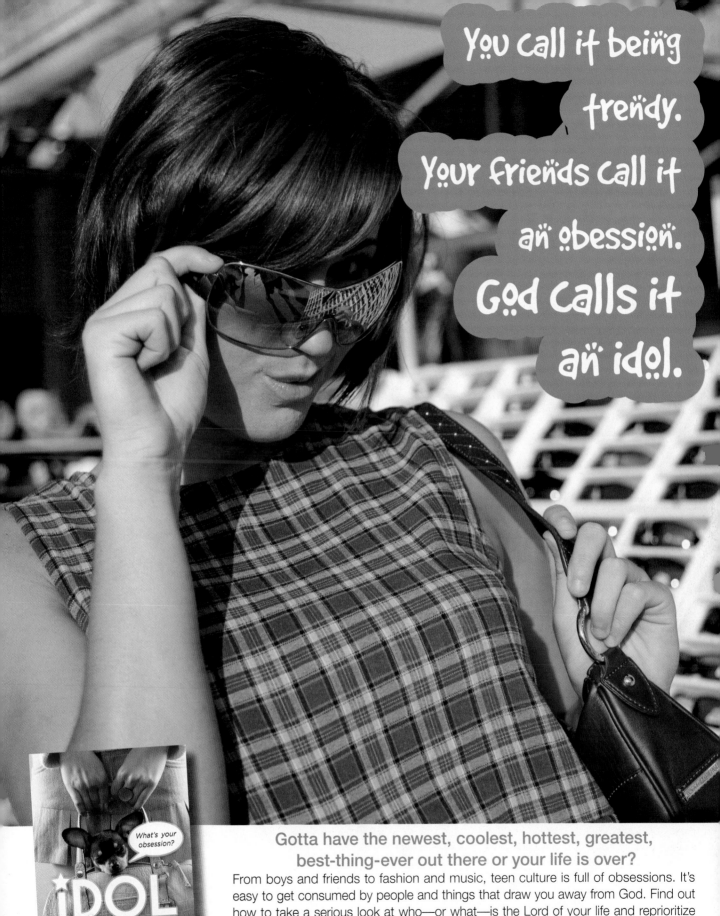

You call it being trendy. Your friends call it an obession. God calls it an idol.

Gotta have the newest, coolest, hottest, greatest, best-thing-ever out there or your life is over?

From boys and friends to fashion and music, teen culture is full of obsessions. It's easy to get consumed by people and things that draw you away from God. Find out how to take a serious look at who—or what—is the Lord of your life and reprioritize your values to keep God at the center of it.

What's your obsession?

IDOL GIRLS

HAYLEY DiMARCO

Bestselling author of *Mean Girls*, *Sexy Girls* and *Technical Virgin*

Hungry Planet
www.hungryplanet.net

Revell
www.revellbooks.com

Available at bookstores everywhere

depression
getting rid of the blues

Depression is often a frequent occurrence in the life of a teenage girl, so first of all, don't freak out like you're some kind of nut case or something. 'Cuz you're not. Most of the time depression will pass on its own, but sometimes it requires some extra soul work. Here are some things for you to think about if you are adrift in a sea of depression and fear drowning in your sorrows.

PMS, Anyone?

When's your next period? PMS can be one of the major causes of emotional turmoil in girls. If your period is a week or so away, then you might just be feeling those hormonal changes. If your PMS seems unmanageable or seems to be getting worse, have a chat with your ob-gyn. She might be able to help you make things run a little more smoothly.

P.S.: Don't eat any chocolate or any kind of sugar the week before your period. It just makes you more agitated. You are probably craving it, but if you can say no to yourself, that self-control will have a big payoff in your happiness.

Get Sweaty

If you are depressed, then it's time to get moving. Your hormones can be less destructive if you get more exercise. If you haven't gotten your blood moving in a while, then it's time to move. I know it's hard when you're bummed, but enlist the help of a friend to get you up and doing something active at least once a day. You'll feel tons better once you get going. Exercise will help your body feel better and your mind be more clear. And most of all, it will help you get out of the rut of spending all your time concentrating on how sad you are. If you want to be happy, exercise is a must!

Brain Food

In a lot of cases depression is a sickness of the mind. That means that if you want to get over it, then you have to give your brain something better to eat than its continual diet of "woe is me." Make a list of all the good things in your life and read it every morning before you get out of bed and every night before you go to sleep. Spend time digesting God's Word by not only reading it but also thinking about it. Memorize verses, talk to your friends about God, and give your brain some positive thoughts to ponder. God's Word has in it everything you need for a healthy mind and spirit. As it says in the Bible, "Whatever is true, whatever is noble, whatever is right, whatever is pure, whatever is lovely, whatever is admirable—if anything is excellent or praiseworthy—think about such things" (Philippians 4:8). When you do that, you are sure to find the light at the end of your depression tunnel.

Food, Food, Food

Food is the fuel for life. Seems obvious enough, but if all you're eating is junk, it's no wonder you feel so depressed. The food you eat affects more than your weight; it affects your emotions as well. Lots of sugary or fried foods can leave you feeling sick. They monkey around with your body and don't give it a good chance to flourish. You know about healthy food, and I know it seems impossible to eat well, but at least make an effort to change a meal here and there by adding something fresh like fruit or veggies. Avoid the fries this week and take the sugar out of your diet. If you want to attack your depression, then you've got to take some extreme measures. And don't worry, once you've gotten your emotions back into the happy zone, you can add back some of your favorite junk foods. But try to remember not to go overboard, because you might just end up right back in depressionville.

is it okay to go camping
with my boyfriend?

Dear Hayley,

My boyfriend asked me to go camping with him and his friends. I don't have a tent, so we would just share a tent. We aren't going to sleep in the same sleeping bag, so you don't have to worry about us doing it or anything. I just want to know if it's okay for us to do that or if I shouldn't go. I just don't know what to do. Is it okay for me to go camping with my boyfriend or not?

Summer

Dear Summer,

I think the best way to figure out a question like that is to look at this verse of the Bible: "Among you there must not be even a hint of sexual immorality" (Ephesians 5:3). When it comes to sleeping in the same tent with your bf, do you think there could be any hint of sexual immorality? In other words, if anyone saw you go in together or knew you slept together, could they possibly come to the conclusion that you were fooling around? Might they not believe you when you say you weren't? That's a hint of sexual immorality.

There is also the question of temptation. Jesus says that if a guy even thinks about having sex with a girl, then it's like he's done it (see Matthew 5:28). In other words, he's sinned in his mind.

If you and your guy are in a tent, in your pjs, lying next to each other, what are the chances that he or you will be tempted? Pretty high?

One other thing: do your parents approve? If they're against it, you can't go. Even if they are okay with it, the choice is still really up to you. Who do you want to be? The girl who doesn't put herself in compromising situations that might cause others to stumble, or the girl who just does whatever feels the best at the time? Making decisions like this can be super hard, but always make them with an awareness of what God's Word says. Ignorance of his Word can leave you heartbroken and hurt both physically and spiritually. So consider his Word carefully before you make a choice.

Hayley

what is the
capital of
alberta?
(homework help! mom banned me from using the web!)

Dear Hayley,

My parents won't let me use the Internet because they think it's "dangerous"! But I need to use it to do my homework. It's not like I'm looking at porn or anything. I just need to find out the capital of Alberta; how bad is that? I'm actually texting you this message from my phone since I can't email you. What can I do to convince them that I can handle the World Wide Web?

Mary

Dear Mary,

First off, it's Edmonton. The second largest city in Alberta. And a cool factoid is that they have the biggest mall in North America! Love it! But that's not really the reason you wrote, is it?

Lots of parents are freaked out about the Internet, what with all the creeps that can be found on it, but that's usually because they don't understand the Internet. It sounds like maybe your parents need a little Internet training session. Look at the short course on Internet safety on the next page and then show it to your parents. Make a list of things you are willing to do in order to make them feel better. Like don't ask for a computer in your room but ask to use one in a family area like the kitchen or living room, where they can always see what you are doing online. Talk to them about getting Internet safety software that can block out a lot of bad sites and pop-ups. It's important for them to see that you are being mature and exploring the safety issues and not ignoring them or saying you can handle it. The best way to convince them that you *can* handle it is by showing them that you understand the dangers and want to be safe. Working on the Internet is a great way to study and learn and can definitely help you with your homework, but if they still say no, then you'll have to wait before you can surf. Just keep proving to them that you are aware of the dangers and willing to do what it takes to protect yourself.

By the way, you can always do research the old-fashioned way and go to the public library. Sure, not as convenient, but they've got everything you need both in print and on the computer.

Hayley

How Do I Stay Safe Online?
10 Ways to Show Your Parents You're Serious about Online Safety

1. Until you build enough trust (or move away to college), keep the computer in an open family area, not in your room.
2. Agree to content filtering software like Bsafe Online or another program that filters out porn.
3. If you have a MySpace, Facebook, Xanga, or blog, tell your parents about it and expect them to read it.
4. Set your profile on social community websites to "Private" so only people you know can access your pages.
5. Never use or post your last name, digits, address, or workplace on any website or in an email or IM to someone you don't know or your parents don't know.
6. Don't use language online that you wouldn't use in front of your parents. If they see you're a different person online, *poof!* The trust is gone.
7. Agree to an "online curfew" so your parents don't have to worry about where you're at (online) after they go to bed.
8. If you know more than your parents about the Web, sit down with them on multiple occasions and get them comfortable with it before you start asking for your freedom.
9. Don't whine about your lack of freedom. Whining doesn't sound mature, and that's what your parents are wondering about—is she mature enough to handle it?
10. If you mess up, admit it. If your parents bust you on a site you shouldn't have been on, don't lie about it. Own it and take your lumps. The quicker you do that, the sooner you'll earn back that trust.

turning the tables

This is the part where I get to turn the tables and ask you the questions. There was a lot of stuff to digest in these pages. I hope you found some things that are gonna make your life better. Hopefully you could relate to some of the questions you read and got inspiration from the knowledge that you aren't alone in this big world. Lots of other girls are struggling with the same things you are struggling with. Being part of a bigger picture is a comforting thing. It's nice to know there is more to life than your present drama and that you aren't a freak of nature, but just a normal human being who's living life.

So here's my Q for you today: Who are you trying to please? Think about it. Who do you think about when you get dressed in the morning? Why do you do the things you do or don't do? Whose approval do you really, really want? Or whose attention? What do you spend most of your time thinking about? The answer to those questions will tell you a lot about yourself and what (or who) is most important to you.

You see, you are the sum total of your thoughts. What you think about most of the time is really who you are. If you think about dancing most of the time then you are probably a dancer. If you think about skating most of the time then I bet you're a skater. Whatever occupies your mind defines who you are, what you do, and how you act. So think about it. What are the things or people who are most often on your mind? Do you think about all your friends most of the day?

A certain guy? A favorite TV show? A sport? A hobby?

When you look at your thoughts and see where they are mostly focused, you start to answer the question about who you are trying to please. Do you think about what you think about most of the time in order to please yourself? Or is it to please your parents, your friends, or your God? What does that answer say about who you are?

One of my favorite verses that I memorized so that I could think of it whenever I need it is Galatians 1:10, "Am I now trying to win the approval of men, or of God? Or am I trying to please men? If I were still trying to please men, I would not be a servant of Christ."

It can get kinda overwhelming when you're trying to please others, because they aren't always pleased. And when that happens your world can come crumbling down. But if your sights aren't set on pleasing others but on pleasing God, then things get less complicated. Sure it's hard to be faithful, but God doesn't dump you or hit you. He doesn't spread rumors about you or yell at you. He's always forgiving, always loving, and always on your side.

So check yourself. What do you think about the most? What is your focus in life? If it isn't God and pleasing him, then you are in for a world of hurt, if not today then one day soon. Choosing to make God your focus and the one whose opinion really counts is a freeing move. And though it might seem ominous, I promise you that it will be the best move you've ever made.

Start today to take an inventory of your thoughts. Get a notebook or journal and write down each hour what you were thinking about. Don't make it long sentences, just summarize like this:

Being accepted

Getting skinny

Finding a parking place

Getting into choir

Bobby

Bobby

Bobby

My friend's drama

Bobby

Etc.

Then after a week look back over it and see where your attention lies. Do you want to change who you are? Then change what you think about. Here's a sample of someone who changed dramatically:

OLD ME

Worried about what to wear

Tried to figure out how to pay my rent

Worried about future

Cried about not having a man

Lonely thoughts

NEW ME

Studied God's Word

Enjoyed family

Planned my future

Rested and enjoyed nature

Thanked God for all he's given me

Yep, that's me. I used to be a worry freak. All my thoughts were on worry. And then I decided to change. I got my thoughts going in a different direction. And now my life is rosier. It wasn't an easy job, but I'm glad I committed to it 'cuz I was going downhill fast. I hope that this exercise does a lot for you. I hope that after taking a good inventory you will decide to change what you think about and who you are trying to please. Turn toward God, find out what he wants you to think about—good thoughts, great thoughts—and find a way to get there.

Can't wait to hear from you again and see all that's going on in your life. Stay in touch on www.askhayley.com. Your Q might make the next issue and you'll be a star! Thanks for taking the journey! And God bless your socks off!

Hayley

REAL ANSWERS FOR TODAY'S TEEN

ask hayley

VOL.3

Bestselling author Hayley DiMarco answers your questions!

I need a later curfew! - How late is too late?

Is playing sports on Sunday OK?

Why do my parents hate my boyfriend?

Will I ever use algebra?!

New girl at school - How do I fit in?

Should I only go to a Christian college?

Help! My boyfriend is transferring schools.

Homeschooler wants to go public - How do I tell

Available July '08

TNGN Teen Issues
10: 0-8007-3236-7
978-0-8007-3236-3
51299
9 780800 732363